american desserts

american

WAYNE HARLEY BRACHMAN

desserts

THE GREATEST SWEETS ON EARTH

Clarkson Potter/Publishers
New York

Published by Clarkson Potter/Publishers, New York, New York.
Member of the Crown Publishing Group, a division of Random House, Inc.
www.randomhouse.com

CLARKSON N. POTTER is a trademark and POTTER and colophon are registered trademarks of Random House, Inc.

Printed in the United States of America

Design by Jane Treuhaft

Library of Congress Cataloging-in-Publication Data
Brachman, Wayne Harley.
    American desserts: the greatest sweets on earth / Wayne Harley Brachman.
1. Desserts.   I. Title.
    TX773 .B69697   2003
641.8'6—dc21   2003006029

ISBN 1-4000-4665-3

10 9 8 7 6 5 4 3 2 1

First Edition

FOR violet mae

Your great-grandpa Sam came to America to find freedom.
The cake was pretty good, too.

contents

red, white & blueberry
DESSERTS

The United States is the home of the foodie as well as the home of the brave. We have the greatest chefs in the world and the most savvy diners, but the pride of Old Glory is our desserts. America is often referred to as the great melting pot, but a more appropriate cooking utensil would probably be a cake pan or a cookie sheet. Walk along any *rue* in Paris and you will see *le brownie,* proudly displayed in the patisseries. Today, even the French pay homage to the apple crisp. American desserts are just the best in the universe!

There is nothing new about this tradition of great desserts in America. When the Pilgrims arrived at Plymouth Rock, they encountered Native Americans who had an incredibly diverse diet but, because few natural sweeteners were available, had almost no concept of dessert. This would change soon after the first course of the first Thanksgiving dinner. It was a whortleberry pudding.

Since then, generations of immigrants have brought their recipes and skills, and a sweet tooth or two, to expand the repertoire of American desserts. Germans contributed *kuchen,* which evolved into Dutch apple pies. From the Dutch came *kookjes* (cookies) and *oliekocken* (doughnuts). Russian Jews brought rugelach and cheesecakes. Italians brought cannoli and Africans smuggled in sesame seeds, which were turned into benne wafers. All of them found a spirit of creative cooking where ideas were not only shared but embellished.

As I researched this book I unearthed and tested hundreds of old American dessert recipes. Many had once been extremely popular but for one reason or another had fallen out of favor. The more I tested, the more puzzled I became at the way they had slipped into obscurity. Time after time, what appeared to be odd-ball ingredients produced the most delectable results. Baking techniques that seemed simple and predictable resulted in the most surprisingly luscious textures. Over and over, I was delighted by just how different and delicious the desserts turned out to be. Chess pie wasn't just a cornmeal custard in a crust, but had a texture all its own. Applesauce Pie (page 70) had a flavor like nothing I had ever tasted. Vinegar Pie (page 46) was absolutely scrumptious. The luscious German's (not German) chocolate cake (see page 113) was made in a most fascinating method. Benne Wafers (page 198) and Molasses "Cry Baby" Lace Cookies (page 201) exploded with rich, exotic flavor. I had to ask myself: Are we really abandoning our culinary heritage or do we just need some reminders of how rich and delicious it really is? I found myself on a mission to revive an amazingly yummy tradition that is in danger of extinction.

Throughout my career as a pastry chef I have been enamored of American desserts. I felt the time was right to rework the best of these classic recipes in modern versions, geared for today's kitchens. This cookbook shows how the ingredients, traditions and ingenuity of generations of American immigrants and pioneers went into a big mixing bowl, and came out as desserts that are unrivaled on any continent. Though some have evolved over the decades, adapting to changing times and tastes, they remain, to my taste, the greatest sweets on earth.

SOME HELPFUL HINTS

All of the recipes in this book were created specifically for the home cook and require only readily available bakeware and equipment. That said, there are major differences in the ways that a professional pastry chef and a home baker approach a recipe, and it pays to take a few tips from the pros. In the pro kitchen, we always assemble our ingredients and get as much as possible ready before we begin any actual cooking. You don't want to be peeling apples or sifting flour when your oven timer is ringing and your sauce is boiling over. We also try to make as many of the components as possible (such as doughs, pie shells, prepared fruits and fillings) ahead of time. This makes the final assembly of the dessert much easier. If a recipe looks too complicated, we break it down into its simplest steps. This way, no single procedure becomes too daunting. Here are some general hints to ensure the best results from your baking efforts:

★ **Slightly softened, pliable butter is often needed for cakes, cookies and some tart doughs. If your recipe calls for butter at room temperature, remember to take it out of the refrigerator several hours in advance.**

★ **Many recipes in this book use liquors, liqueurs or other alcoholic beverages as flavoring agents. In most cases, the alcohol gets "cooked out" but small traces may still remain. If this is a concern, you can always omit the alcoholic flavoring or substitute white grape juice or another fruit juice.**

★ **Lightly toasting nuts adds a world of flavor to them. Preheat your oven to 325°F., spread the nuts on a cookie sheet and bake for 5 minutes, turning the cookie sheet around midway through baking. (Because of their high oil content, peanuts, cashews, macadamias and Brazil nuts are difficult to roast at home. They cook from the inside out so the centers can burn before the outside shows any color. Also, residual heat keeps cooking them for several minutes after they are removed from the oven. It is best to purchase them already roasted.)**

★ **Toasting dried, shredded coconut is also a great flavor booster: Follow the same procedure as for toasting nuts but stir the coconut with a spoon midway through baking. The best shredded coconut is the unsweetened type that is sold in health food stores and Asian markets.**

★ The rich, deep oak flavor of a Jamaican rum (such as Meyer's, Appleton's, or Corruba brands) can add a whole level of flavor to many desserts. I believe it should be in every pantry, right next to the vanilla extract.

★ Carpenters have a saying: measure it twice, cut it once. This applies just as well to baking—accurate measuring is half the battle in making a good dessert. Measure dry ingredients by scooping them up in measuring spoons or dry measuring cups. Level them off with the back of a knife. If a recipe calls for a $1/2$ cup of an ingredient, use a $1/2$ cup measure. (You can't get an accurate reading by filling the dry ingredients halfway up in a 1 cup measure.) Measure liquids in clear measuring cups. Always bend down and read the fill line at eye level. Measure brown sugar by lightly tamping it down into a dry measuring cup.

★ Even when a cake pan, pie dish or tart pan is the exact diameter that a recipe calls for, the depth can still vary. So never fill a cake pan more than halfway up. With the exception of apple pies, do not fill a pie or tart shell higher than its rim before baking. And it's always a good idea to put a rimmed baking sheet under your cake, pie or tart to catch any possible spillovers in the oven.

Basic Pie Shell ★ Basic Tart Shell ★ Chocolate Crumb Crust ★ Classic Apple Pie ★ Dutch Apple Pie ★ Cherry Pie ★ Blueberry Crumb Pie ★ Peach Pie ★ Nectarine Pie ★ Strawberry-Rhubarb Pie with Lattice Top ★ Pineapple Pie with Macadamia Crumb Topping ★ Cranberry-Walnut Pie ★ Pecan Pie ★ Maple Walnut Pie ★ Shoofly Pie ★ Vinegar Pie ★ Osgood or Jefferson Davis Pie ★ Pumpkin Pie with Ginger-Graham Crust ★ Sweet Potato Pie ★ Key Lime Tart with Coconut Macaroon Crust ★ Chess Pie ★ Lemon Meringue Pie ★ Vanilla Malted Custard Pie ★ Coconut Custard Pie ★ Lemon Chiffon Pie ★ Eggnog Chiffon Pie ★ Chocolate Custard Pie ★ Banana Cream Pie ★ Applesauce Pie ★ Classic Missisippi Mud Pie ★ Raspberry "Queen of the Mississippi" Mud Pie ★ Baked Black Bottom Pie ★ Chocolate Pudding Black Bottom Pie

pies, tarts

& ALL SORTS OF FILLINGS

From Mom's apple specialty to "Bye Bye Miss You-know-who," pie has been a superstar of the American kitchen since Colonial times, perhaps the most iconic representation of American dessert making. The Pilgrims started to bake pies the moment they disembarked at Plymouth Rock, cooking them up over an open hearth in heavy iron kettles called Dutch ovens. Later, when these kettles were supplemented by true ovens, pies were so crucial a part of the diet that ovens were often rated by how many pies they could hold. Pie was eaten at any time of the day, but especially at breakfast. It wasn't long before Colonial bakers were augmenting their repertoire of pies with new recipes created from ingredients of the New World, begetting corn, pumpkin, rhubarb and cranberry pies.

This creative spirit continued to inspire bakers as the great adventure of American pie baking went forward. Regional variations and specialties popped up all over the new nation. Southern cooks dreamed up chess pies and pecan pies, which kept well in their hot, humid climate. Up north, resourceful Yankees scoured the pantry to create applesauce, maple-walnut and even cracker-based mock apple pies. During long winters, bakers took advantage of the available dairy supply to make creamy custard-filled pies. Across the country, bakers seized any excuse to come up with a new pie recipe; pies were invented to honor local dignitaries like Jefferson Davis and even to serve as decoys to lure flies.

With the advance of the industrial revolution, modern conveniences like electric mixers and refrigeration gave birth to airy chiffon pies and chilled custard fillings. Even in the post–World War II period, when homemakers sought out shiny, modern labor-saving gadgets and newfangled instant ingredients, the old-fashioned art of pie making managed to persevere as one of the most creative aspects of American cookery.

Ubiquitous as pies are, making them can still seem very intimidating. There is an art to working with the pastry, assembling the components and putting them together, and getting the top and bottom crusts to cook simultaneously. Don't let that scare you off; with a little practice, you'll soon find them as easy as you-know-what.

There are two types of prebaked pie or tart shells:

BLIND BAKED PIE OR TART SHELL This shell is partially baked. Liquid fillings, such as custards, can then be poured into it without turning the dough all soggy. The filled pie or tart is then gently baked until the filling sets and the crust bakes thoroughly and crisps.

1. Preheat the oven to 400°F., arranging a rack in the middle position.

2. Line the shell with aluminum foil and weight it down with dried beans or pie weights. Bake at 400°F. for 12 minutes. Remove the aluminum foil and reduce the temperature to 350°F. Bake the shell for 4 more minutes, or until the pastry is slightly dry on the surface.

FULLY BAKED PIE OR TART SHELL This shell will be crisp and ready for a cooked filling such as pastry cream, pudding or curd. Once the shell is filled, the pie will be ready to serve.

1. Preheat the oven to 400°F., arranging a rack in the middle position.

2. Line the shell with aluminum foil and weight it down with dried beans or pie weights. Bake at 400°F. for 12 minutes. Remove the aluminum foil and reduce the temperature to 350°F. Bake the shell for 10 more minutes, or until the pastry is golden brown.

CRIMPING is a method for finishing off the edges of a single pie crust or for sealing together the top and bottom crusts of a double pie crust.

Step 1. Fit the dough into the pie pan, lightly pressing it against the sides of the pan with your fingertips.

Step 2. Tuck the overhang under itself so that it extends $\frac{1}{4}$ inch over the edge of the pan.

Step 3. While pulling the dough outward with the thumb and index finger of one hand, pull it in with the index finger of the other hand.

Step 4. Continue, at 2-inch intervals, around the circumference of the pie shell.

Additional shell recipes appear throughout the book:
Coconut Macaroon Crust, page 55
Lattice Top, page 34
Heart Crust, page 26
Cheddar Cheese Pie Shell, page 71
Chocolate Shell, page 72
Ginger Graham Crust, page 50
Coconut Graham Crust, page 56

PIE TIPS

Making pies is a lot easier when you don't try to tackle everything at once. Making the dough in advance is a great way to get a head start. You can wrap and refrigerate several portions of dough for up to 5 days. Unbaked pie shells will keep in the freezer for up to 6 weeks. Defrost them in the refrigerator or, for blind baked or fully baked shells, pop them directly into the oven and bake straight from the freezer.

★ **Butter makes a flavorful dough but lard or vegetable shortening make the flakiest crusts. Crisp tarts shells are best when made with butter only. Tender, flaky pie crusts benefit from a combination of shortenings.**

★ **To see if there is enough water in your dough, pick up a handful and gently squeeze it into a ball. It should hold together.**

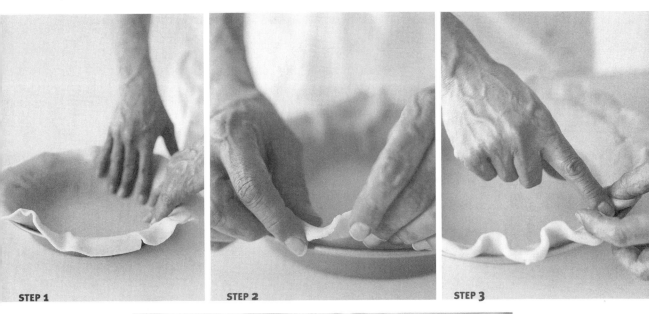

STEP 1

STEP 2

STEP 3

CRIMPING

STEP 4

★ Don't overmix your dough. Small bits of butter and shortening in the dough are not only fine, but actually preferred.

★ Chill out! Keep your ingredients cold, especially butter and shortening. Cold hinders the formation of gluten (a kind of protein that makes dough tough and chewy) and helps to keep the crust tender and flaky.

★ Roll dough in one direction at a time, using long, even strokes and lifting the pin at the end of each pass. This way, the butter or shortening will be layered into the dough, resulting in a flaky crust. Short, back-and-forth motions will just result in a scrunched-up mess with the texture of cardboard.

★ Stop rolling just before you reach the edges of the dough. This will prevent it from getting too thin at the edges.

★ To keep your dough from sticking, dust your rolling pin and rolling surface with flour. In warm weather, roll dough out early in the day, when it is cooler.

★ Dried beans or cherry pits make great pie weights for baking an unfilled pie shell.

★ Even when a pie pan is the exact diameter that a recipe calls for, the depth can still vary. This affects both the size of the crust that fits into the pan and the volume of filling it can hold. So, except for apple pies, do not fill a pie or tart shell higher than its rim before baking.

★ Always put a tray or cookie sheet under your pie to catch any drips. Who needs to clean up a big burnt mess in the oven?

★ If your top crust is browning too quickly, set a foil tent over the pie. You can also try placing a cookie sheet on a rack just above it.

BASIC pie shell

$\frac{1}{4}$ cup plus 2 tablespoons vegetable shortening

1 cup (2 sticks) cold unsalted butter, cut into pea-size bits

3 cups pastry or all-purpose flour

1. Scoop $\frac{1}{2}$-teaspoon balls of shortening and drop them onto a sheet of waxed paper or parchment set on a baking sheet. Freeze for at least 30 minutes, until rock hard.

2. In a large bowl, using a mixer with the flat paddle attachment, a pastry blender or your fingertips, work the butter into the flour until the mixture is lumpy. Work in the cold shortening balls until the mixture looks like coarse meal. Sprinkle on $\frac{1}{4}$ cup of ice water, a bit at a time, working in just enough to make the dough come together in a ball. Divide the ball in half and pat each half into a $\frac{3}{4}$-inch-thick disk. Wrap each disk tightly in plastic wrap and refrigerate for at least 2 hours, or overnight.

3. Unwrap a disk, and on a lightly floured surface, roll the dough into a 12-inch circle about $\frac{1}{8}$ inch thick. Fit the dough into a 9-inch pie pan.

For a single-crust pie: Tuck any overhanging dough under itself so it extends by $\frac{1}{4}$ inch around the edge of the pie plate. Crimp the edges (see page 16). Set the unbaked shell in the refrigerator for 30 minutes to rest, then in the freezer for at least 30 minutes to harden before filling and baking. (You may also wrap the unbaked shell tightly in plastic wrap and freeze it for up to 6 weeks.)

For blind baked and fully baked shells: Follow the instructions on page 15.

For a double-crust pie: Set the unbaked bottom shell in the refrigerator for 30 minutes to rest, then in the freezer for at least 30 minutes to harden, if desired. (You may also wrap the unbaked shell tightly in plastic wrap and freeze it for up to 6 weeks.) Roll the second disk $\frac{1}{8}$ inch thick for the top crust and chill for at least 30 minutes.

And just who was it who first said "...as easy as pie"?

Absolutely nobody! The original phrase was "as easy as eating pie." Somewhere along the line it was changed to the present phrase.

BASIC tart shell

Tarts are French and pies are American but in recent times it has become de rigueur to pack a tart shell with an all-American filling. In many cases, the pairing works. As a matter of fact, some very traditional pies, such as Pecan (page 40) and Banana Cream (page 68), truly benefit from a crisp change of crust. This tart dough is not the crunchy pâte sucrée type, but a very flaky pâte brisée. The smearing method used when making this dough is one the French call fraisage. *It helps to layer the butter and flour, producing a very flaky tart crust.*

MAKES ONE 9¹/₂-INCH TART SHELL

1¹/₂ cups all-purpose flour
1 tablespoon granulated sugar
¹/₂ cup (1 stick) cold unsalted butter, cut into pea-size bits
1 egg beaten with 1 cup ice water
Nonstick vegetable-oil spray

1. Stir the flour and sugar together in a large bowl. Using a mixer with the flat paddle attachment, a pastry blender or your fingertips, work the butter into the flour until the mixture resembles coarse meal. Sprinkle on the eggy water, bit by bit, working in just enough to make the dough come together in a ball (about 3 or 4 tablespoons).

2. On a lightly floured surface, divide the dough into walnut-size pieces and, with the heel of your hand, smear each piece away from you into a 6-inch streak. Scrape the dough up and gather it into a 9-inch disk. Wrap in plastic wrap and refrigerate for at least 2 hours, or overnight.

3. Lightly coat a 9¹/₂-inch tart pan with a removable bottom with nonstick vegetable-oil spray. On a lightly floured surface, roll the dough into an 11¹/₂-inch circle about 3/16 inch thick. Fit the dough into the tart pan and trim the edges, leaving a 1-inch overhang. Tuck the overhanging dough under itself to reinforce the sides. Set the unbaked shell in the refrigerator for 30 minutes to rest, then in the freezer for at least 30 minutes to harden before filling and baking. (You may also wrap it and freeze it for up to 6 weeks.)

chocolate crumb CRUST

Here's a fun crust that works in just about any recipe that calls for a fully baked pie shell.

MAKES ONE 9-INCH PIE SHELL

6 tablespoons unsalted butter, melted
**1½ cups chocolate wafer or dried chocolate cake crumbs (pulverized in a food
  processor)**
¼ cup granulated sugar

1. Brush the bottom and sides of a 9-inch pie pan with 2 teaspoons of the butter.

2. In a medium bowl, mix together the chocolate crumbs, sugar and the rest of the melted butter. Pat the mixture firmly over the bottom and up the sides of the pan in an even layer. Refrigerate for at least 30 minutes.

3. Preheat the oven to 350°F., arranging a rack in the middle position.

4. Bake the crust for 8 to 10 minutes, until set and dry. Cool on a rack before filling.

BAKER'S NOTEBOOK

This crust can be kept, unbaked and lightly wrapped in plastic wrap, for 2 days in the refrigerator or 6 weeks in the freezer.

CLASSIC apple pie

A crust that's crisp on top and set on the bottom, filling that's moist and gooey, with fruit that's tender but still has a bit of bite—that's what makes a perfect apple pie. Mastering this American icon is easy if you have a few tricks up your sleeve. Just follow these simple instructions for the quintessential American pie.

MAKES ONE 9-INCH PIE

1 double-crust Basic Pie Shell (page 19), unbaked and chilled

APPLE FILLING
$3/4$ cup thawed apple juice concentrate
$1/4$ cup cornstarch
$1/2$ cup lightly packed light brown sugar
$1/4$ teaspoon ground cinnamon
1 teaspoon dark rum
1 teaspoon vanilla extract
$2^{1}/_{2}$ pounds (7 or 8) tart, medium baking apples, such as Granny Smith, Rome, Golden Delicious or Northern Spy, peeled, cored and cut into 12 pieces each (about 6 cups)

Egg wash: 1 large egg white mixed with 2 tablespoons water
2 teaspoons Demerara, coarse-grain or granulated sugar, for sprinkling

1. Preheat the oven to 400°F., arranging a rack in the middle position.

2. Make the Apple Filling: In a medium saucepan, whisk together the apple juice concentrate and cornstarch. Let rest for 1 minute, then whisk in the brown sugar, cinnamon, rum and vanilla. Cook over medium heat, whisking constantly, for 3 minutes, until thick and bubbling (it should look fairly clear and gel-like). Transfer to a large bowl and stir in the apples.

3. Mound the filling into the bottom pie shell. Moisten the edges of the crust with water. Drape on the top crust and press the edges of the dough together to seal. Tuck the outer circumference of the dough under itself so it extends $1/4$ inch around the edge of the pie pan. Crimp the edges together (see page 16).

"Spit in my ears and tell me no lies, but give me no dried-apple pies." —Old Nebraska saying

4. With a pastry brush, paint the top crust with a light coating of the egg wash. Sprinkle on the Demerara sugar. With a sharp knife or scissors, slash 5 little steam vents in the crust.

5. Bake at 400°F. for 35 minutes. Reduce the oven temperature to 350°F. and bake for 25 minutes longer, until the top crust is golden and the filling is bubbling. Transfer to a rack to cool.

VARIATION

APPLE-BERRY PIE Add ½ pint of fresh or frozen raspberries, blackberries, marionberries or cranberries to the filling mixture.

NOTEBOOK

BAKER'S

Most apples must be kept in acidulated water (lemon juice + H_2O) after peeling or they will turn brown. Unfortunately, this causes them to soak up a lot of water, which dilutes their flavor and can also turn the bottom pie crust into a soggy mess. I also find the flavor of lemon to be unwelcome in an apple pie. It fights against the natural flavor of the apple. That's why I prefer tart Granny Smiths for all-purpose baking, and especially for pies. You can peel them in advance and, because they contain so much natural acid, you never have to put them in acidulated water after they are peeled.

dutch APPLE PIE

The Dutch settlers of Nieuw Amsterdam (that's New York to you and me) brought a strong tradition of pastry making to the New World. In 1656, they established America's first public bakery where they could produce Madeira and caraway kookjes *(cookies) and their beloved streusel-topped apple cake. But as popular as this cake was, it still managed to be reinterpreted in the form of a pie—chock-full of apples and raisins and topped with a crunchy cinnamon streusel—and that turned out to be the keeper.*

MAKES ONE 9-INCH PIE

DUTCH APPLE FILLING
1¼ cups thawed apple juice concentrate
¼ cup cornstarch
¼ cup lightly packed dark brown sugar
1 teaspoon dark rum
1 teaspoon vanilla extract
½ cup golden raisins
1¾ pounds (about 5) tart, medium baking apples, such as Granny Smith,
    Rome, Golden Delicious or Northern Spy, peeled, cored and cut into eighths
    (about 5 cups)

CINNAMON STREUSEL
1 cup all-purpose flour
½ cup lightly packed dark brown sugar
1 teaspoon ground cinnamon
6 tablespoons unsalted butter, cut into pea-size bits

1 single-crust Basic Pie Shell (page 19), blind baked (see page 15)

1. Make the Dutch Apple Filling: In a medium saucepan, whisk together the apple juice concentrate and cornstarch. Let rest for 1 minute, then whisk in the brown sugar, rum and vanilla. Cook over medium heat, whisking constantly, for 3 minutes, until thick and bubbling (it should look fairly clear and gel-like). Transfer to a large bowl and stir in the raisins and apples.

2. Preheat the oven to 375°F., arranging a rack in the middle position.

3. Make the Cinnamon Streusel: In a medium bowl, combine the flour, brown sugar, and cinnamon. Work in the butter, rubbing and pinching it with your fingers until the mixture looks mealy and lumpy. Don't overwork it to the point that it becomes sticky. Set aside in a cool place until ready to use.

4. Mound the apple filling into the prepared shell. Cover the filling completely with the streusel. Bake at 375°F. for 40 minutes, until the streusel is browned and the filling is bubbling. Transfer to a rack to cool.

VARIATION

DUTCH APPLE-CHERRY PIE Substitute dried sour cherries for the raisins.

In the early 1800s, John Chapman, aka Johnny Appleseed, picked up a hoe and left Massachusetts to plant apple orchards throughout the Ohio River Valley. A vegetarian and disciple of the Swedish mystic Emanuel Swedenborg, he preached the gospel as he scattered apple seeds. He was also one of America's first, and most notorious, fashion victims. He sported a coffee sack as a shirt and donned a saucepan as a hat. Apple trees are usually grown from grafts, but Chapman considered this method to be sinful. Go figure.

cherry PIE

A crust of overlapping hearts makes a novel (and absolutely adorable) way to top a cherry pie. IQF (individually quick frozen) cherries taste just about as good as the fresh stuff and are infinitely easier to work with. Avoid canned cherries. You can make a pie with them but it will taste more of tin and sugar than anything else.

MAKES ONE 9-INCH PIE

1 double-crust Basic Pie Shell (page 19), unbaked and chilled

CHERRY FILLING
One 12-ounce package of frozen sour cherries (preferably IQF), thawed, juice
    drained and reserved, or see Baker's Notebook below for fresh cherries
2 tablespoons brandy
3 tablespoons granulated sugar
2 tablespoons cornstarch

Egg wash: 1 large egg white mixed with 2 tablespoons water
2 teaspoons Demerara, coarse-grain or granulated sugar, for sprinkling

1. With a heart-shaped cookie cutter (or several in different sizes) cut out as many heart shapes as possible from the top unbaked crust. Use a metal spatula to transfer the dough hearts to a waxed paper–lined cookie sheet and refrigerate for 15 minutes.

2. Make the Cherry Filling: In a medium saucepan, whisk together the juice from the cherries, the brandy, sugar and cornstarch. Let rest for 1 minute and whisk again. Cook over medium heat, whisking constantly, until thick and bubbling. Allow it to bubble for 10 seconds. (It should look fairly clear and gel-like.) Remove from the heat and stir in the cherries. Set aside to cool to room temperature, about 30 minutes.

3. Preheat the oven to 400°F., arranging a rack in the middle position.

4. Mound the filling into the bottom pie shell, taking care not to get any on the rim. Paint the rim with egg wash and attach a ring of hearts to it, with the tips of the hearts pointing in. Paint them with egg wash. Add another concentric ring of hearts inside the first, over-lapping the first ring slightly, and paint with egg wash. Continue until you reach the center, leaving spaces here and there for steam to escape. Coat with a final layer of egg wash and sprinkle with Demerara sugar.

5. Bake at 400°F. for 20 minutes. Reduce the oven temperature to 350°F. and bake for 15 more minutes, until the top crust is golden and the filling is bubbling. Transfer to a rack to cool.

NOTEBOOK

BAKER'S

To make a traditional double-crust cherry pie, follow the instructions for Classic Apple Pie (page 22), substituting the Cherry Filling for the Apple Filling.

This pie can also be made with 6 cups of pitted, fresh sour cherries. Sour cherries are available at farm stands and specialty fruit stores only briefly, usually at the beginning of summer. After pitting, let them soak in ½ cup of sugar for 1 hour to draw out their juices. Then stir in ¼ cup of water.

In 1833, E. D. Lay and his brother Z. K. started a plant nursery in Ypsilanti, Michigan, that now bears their name. The fruits of their labor are the orchards that grow around Lake Michigan, where 75 percent of America's sour cherries are picked. The densest concentration of cherry trees in the world (22,600 trees per square mile) is in the area around Traverse City.

BLUEBERRY crumb pie

Spruce up your blueberry pie with a little port wine. It makes the blueberry flavor just explode.

MAKES ONE 9-INCH PIE OR 9$\frac{1}{2}$-INCH TART

BLUEBERRY FILLING

1 cup port wine

$\frac{1}{2}$ cup granulated sugar

1 teaspoon vanilla extract

$\frac{1}{4}$ cup cornstarch

2 pints fresh blueberries, rinsed in cold water and drained

STREUSEL TOPPING

1 cup all-purpose flour

$\frac{1}{2}$ cup lightly packed dark brown sugar

6 tablespoons unsalted butter, cut into pea-size bits

1 single-crust Basic Pie Shell (page 19) or Basic Tart Shell (page 20),
     blind baked (see page 15)

1. Make the Blueberry Filling: Combine $\frac{3}{4}$ cup of the port with the sugar in a large saucepan. Bring to a boil and cook over high heat for 3 minutes to evaporate some of the alcohol. Meanwhile, in a small bowl, whisk together the remaining $\frac{1}{4}$ cup of port, the vanilla and cornstarch. Add to the saucepan and, whisking constantly, cook over medium heat for 1 more minute, until very thick and clear. Remove from heat and stir in the blueberries.

2. Preheat the oven to 375°F., arranging a rack in the middle position.

3. Make the Streusel Topping: In a medium bowl, combine the flour and brown sugar. Work in the butter, rubbing and pinching it with your fingers until the mixture looks mealy and lumpy. Don't overwork it to the point that it becomes sticky. Set aside in a cool place until ready to use.

4. Spoon the blueberry filling into the prepared shell. Cover the filling completely with the streusel. Bake at 375°F. for 30 minutes, or until the streusel is browned and the filling is bubbling. Transfer to a rack to cool.

VARIATION

PECAN STREUSEL TOPPING Follow the above recipe, but in the Streusel Topping, reduce the flour to ³/₄ cup and add ¹/₂ cup coarsely chopped, toasted pecans (see page 10).

BAKER'S NOTEBOOK

When it comes to cooking with port wine, the cheap domestic stuff in the screw-cap bottle is actually better than the ritzy, delicious imported stuff. Fine port is divine for sipping and savoring. For baking, stick with the swill. You won't taste the difference.

Blueberries will tell you when they are perfect. They should be deep blue, firm and partially coated with little droplets of white wax. Soft berries taste flat. If they are reddish, they will be sour. Moldy berries or those with rust spots will, of course, be positively yucky.

peach PIE

If any pie can be described as glorious, peach pie is the one. Although a little vanilla and almond extract will add depth to the flavor of your pie, perfectly picked and ripened peaches don't need any help from the extract bottle. But peach pie can be tricky. The important thing is to move quickly: Fill, top and crimp as fast as you can, then get that pie into a hot oven. Peaches exude a lot of juice and, unless your filling thickens up quickly, you can end up with a bottom crust that's as soggy as a Georgia swamp.

MAKES ONE 9-INCH PIE

1 double-crust Basic Pie Shell (page 19), unbaked and chilled

PEACH FILLING
3 pounds (8 or 9) ripe peaches
1/2 cup granulated sugar
1/4 cup cornstarch
1/2 teaspoon vanilla extract (optional)
1/4 teaspoon almond extract (optional)

Egg wash: 1 large egg white mixed with 2 tablespoons water
2 teaspoons Demerara, coarse-grain or granulated sugar, for sprinkling

1. Preheat the oven to 400°F., arranging a rack in the middle position.

2. Make the Peach Filling: Bring a large pot of water to a boil. Slice the peaches along their creases and twist them into halves. With a spoon, pry out the pits. In batches of 3 or 4, drop the peach halves into the water and boil for 2 minutes. With a slotted spoon, transfer them to a bowl of ice water. Let cool, then remove from the water and slip the skins off. Slice each half into 3 wedges and place in a large bowl.

3. Sprinkle on the sugar and let sit for 10 minutes.

4. Drain the liquid from the peaches into a small saucepan. Whisk in the cornstarch and the vanilla and almond extracts, if using. Let sit for 30 seconds. While whisking constantly, cook over medium-high heat for 3 minutes, until very thick and clear. Remove from heat and stir this slurry into the peaches.

5. Mound the filling into the bottom pie shell. Moisten the edges of the crust with water. Drape on the top crust and press the edges of the dough together to seal. Tuck the outer circumference of the dough under itself so it extends $\frac{1}{4}$ inch around the edge of the pie pan. Crimp the edges together (see page 16).

6. With a pastry brush, paint the top crust with a light coating of the egg wash. Sprinkle on the Demerara sugar. With a sharp knife or scissors, slash 5 little steam vents in the crust.

7. Bake at 400°F. for 35 minutes. Reduce the oven temperature to 350°F. and bake for 15 minutes longer, or until the top crust is golden and the filling is bubbling. Transfer to a rack to cool.

BAKER'S NOTEBOOK

Peaches come in two varieties, freestone and cling. Although clings are good for eating "out of hand," it is extremely difficult to remove their pits. It is also (unless you are blessed with some mystical ability) impossible to look at a peach and tell what lies beneath its fuzz. Ask your grocer about the pedigree of the peaches you are buying, and choose freestones for easy pitting.

Okay, I know it's sort of cheating and definitely not "by the book," but if you are having a hard time peeling peaches with the standard method listed above, here's an alternative way to peel them without boiling them and getting them all soggy. Just use a vegetable peeler! Follow all of the other instructions for pitting and making the filling.

NECTARINE pie

If you like peach pie, you'll love nectarine pie. Nectarines are easier to pit and since they don't exude as much juice, they don't make the crust as soggy. Unlike peaches, they have ultrathin skins that don't toughen up when they are heated, so you don't even have to peel them.

MAKES ONE 9-INCH PIE

1 double-crust Basic Pie Shell (page 19), unbaked and chilled

NECTARINE FILLING
3 pounds (8 or 9) ripe nectarines
¼ cup cornstarch
½ cup granulated sugar
1 teaspoon vanilla extract

Egg wash: 1 large egg white mixed with 2 tablespoons water
2 teaspoons Demerara, coarse-grain or granulated sugar, for sprinkling

1. Preheat the oven to 400°F., arranging a rack in the middle position.

2. **Make the Nectarine Filling:** Cut each nectarine through its seam and completely slice around the pit. Twist to separate into halves and pluck out the pit. Slice each half into 4 wedges and place in a large bowl.

3. Sprinkle on the cornstarch, sugar and vanilla. Toss to coat the nectarines completely.

4. Mound the filling into the bottom pie shell. Moisten the edges of the crust with water. Drape on the top crust and press the edges of the dough together to seal. Tuck the outer circumference of the dough under itself so it extends ¼ inch around the edge of the pie pan (see page 16).

5. With a pastry brush, paint the top crust with a light coating of the egg wash. Sprinkle on the Demerara sugar. With scissors or a sharp knife, slash 5 little steam vents in the crust.

6. Bake at 400°F. for 35 minutes. Reduce the oven temperature to 350°F. and bake for 15 minutes longer, or until the top crust is golden and the filling is bubbling. Transfer to a rack to cool.

VARIATION

NECTARINE-BERRY PIE Gently fold 1 cup (½ pint) of blueberries, raspberries, blackberries, marionberries or gooseberries into the nectarine filling.

BAKER'S NOTEBOOK

Any fruit pie can be turned into a deep-dish pie. Put the filling into a 2½-quart casserole or baking dish. Roll out a disk of Basic Pie Shell (page 19) to fit the dish, then drape it over the filling. With a sharp knife or scissors, cut 5 slashes in the crust to let out steam. Bake for the recommended time for each recipe. It will be done when the crust is golden brown and the filling is bubbling.

strawberry-rhubarb pie
WITH LATTICE TOP

Fresh rhubarb and early strawberries signal the arrival of springtime, and the combination of the tart vegetable and the sweet berries makes for a perfect pie filling. In Colonial times, rhubarb was such a popular pie filling that it was actually called "pie plant." A word of caution: Always cut off and discard all of the rhubarb leaves, which are poisonous. Green parts of the remaining stalks are fine, but the redder the rhubarb, the tastier. Don' t bother with peeling the rhubarb; you' ll waste the tastiest part. Just wash the stalks well to release any clinging soil.

MAKES ONE 9-INCH PIE

1 double-crust Basic Pie Shell (page 19), unbaked and chilled

STRAWBERRY-RHUBARB FILLING
1 bunch of rhubarb (about a pound), cut into ¹/₂-inch chunks (about 4¹/₂ cups)
³/₄ cup granulated sugar
1 teaspoon vanilla extract
Grated zest of 1 orange (about 2 tablespoons)
¹/₄ cup cornstarch
1 pint strawberries, washed, dried and stemmed

Egg wash: 1 large egg mixed with 2 tablespoons water
Demerara, coarse-grain or granulated sugar, for sprinkling

1. In a large bowl, toss the rhubarb and ¹/₄ cup of the sugar together. Set aside for 1 hour to "sweat out" some of the juices.

2. Make the Lattice Top: Roll the top crust of the double-crust shell into a 10-inch square. With a pizza cutter or a sharp knife, cut the square of dough into twenty ¹/₂-inch-wide strips. Place 8 of these strips on a floured cookie sheet, parallel to each other, perpendicular to you, and ¹/₃ inch apart. Bring the far end of every other strip to meet the end near you; every other strip is now folded in half. Place a new strip of dough horizontally across the 4 unfolded strips, right above where the other strips are folded. Unfold the strips away from

you to cover it. Repeat with the rest of the strips. Turn the pan completely around
180 degrees and repeat the process. Gently press the strips down so they stick together.
Refrigerate for 30 minutes, until firm.

3. Preheat the oven to 400°F., arranging a rack in the middle position.

4. Drain the rhubarb, then toss it with the vanilla, orange zest, cornstarch, remaining
$\frac{1}{2}$ cup sugar and strawberries. Mound the filling into the pie shell.

5. With a pastry brush, paint the edge of the bottom crust with egg wash. Carefully slide
the lattice over the pie. Press down around the rim to seal, then trim the excess dough.
Carefully paint the top lattice with egg wash
and sprinkle with a little sugar.

6. Bake at 400°F. for 20 minutes. Reduce
the oven temperature to 350°F. and bake for
20 minutes longer, or until the filling is
thick and bubbling and the top crust is
golden brown. Transfer to a rack to cool.

BAKER'S NOTEBOOK

Strawberries soak up water when they
are washed. This dilutes their flavor and
adds unwanted liquid to your pie filling.
To minimize this, wash them by dunking
them into a bowl of cold water. Agitate
them to release any sand, then quickly
pull them out. Drain them in a colander
and spread them on paper towels, patting
until completely dry.

PINEAPPLE PIE WITH
macadamia crumb topping

I have heard that pineapple pie is an acquired taste. It's certainly exotic, with a refreshing yet luscious tropical flavor and a deeply intoxicating aroma. A layer of smooth and creamy vanilla pudding and a crunchy topping of macadamia-nut streusel give this pie a texture like no other. So now, what's not to like?

MAKES ONE 9-INCH PIE OR 9^1/$_2$-INCH TART

1 single-crust Basic Pie Shell (page 19) or Basic Tart Shell (page 20),
　　blind baked (see page 15)

VANILLA PUDDING
3 tablespoons cornstarch
1^1/$_2$ cups milk
^{1}/$_4$ cup plus 1 tablespoon granulated sugar
3 large egg yolks
1 teaspoon vanilla extract
1 tablespoon unsalted butter

PINEAPPLE FILLING
1 ripe pineapple
^{1}/$_2$ cup pineapple juice
2 tablespoons dark rum
^{1}/$_4$ cup cornstarch
2 tablespoons unsalted butter
^{1}/$_2$ cup lightly packed dark brown sugar

STREUSEL TOPPING
^{3}/$_4$ cup all-purpose flour
^{1}/$_4$ cup lightly packed dark brown sugar
4 tablespoons unsalted butter, cut into pea-size bits
^{1}/$_4$ cup (1^1/$_4$ ounces) unsalted, coarsely chopped macadamia nuts

1. Make the Vanilla Pudding: In a medium bowl, whisk the cornstarch into $\frac{1}{2}$ cup of the milk. Whisk in $\frac{1}{4}$ cup of the sugar, the egg yolks and vanilla.

2. In a medium saucepan, bring the remaining tablespoon of sugar and the remaining cup of milk to a simmer over medium heat.

3. While gently whisking the egg yolk mixture, slowly drizzle the hot milk mixture into it until completely incorporated. Return the mixture to the saucepan and, while constantly whisking and scraping the bottom of the pot, cook over medium heat until tiny bubbles boil up continuously for 10 seconds. Stir in the butter. Strain into a bowl and cover the surface with parchment or waxed paper. Set aside to cool down, then refrigerate.

4. Make the Pineapple Filling: With a big, sharp knife, cut off and discard the top and bottom of the pineapple. Cut the center into 4 wedges. Slice the tough inner core from each piece. Run a paring knife under each piece to free the flesh from the skin. Cut out any "eyes" that may remain. Cut each piece lengthwise into 3 spears. Cut each spear into $\frac{1}{3}$-inch-thick wedges.

5. In a small bowl, whisk together the pineapple juice, rum and cornstarch and set aside.

6. In a large saucepan or skillet set over medium-high heat, cook and stir the butter and brown sugar until they combine in a smooth syrup, about 30 seconds. Add the pineapple and cook for 2 minutes. Add the cornstarch mixture and cook, stirring, until the liquid is bubbling and thickened. Remove from the heat.

7. Preheat the oven to 350°F., arranging a rack in the middle position.

8. Make the Streusel Topping: In a medium bowl, combine the flour and brown sugar. Work in the butter, rubbing and pinching it with your fingers until the mixture looks mealy and lumpy. Don't overwork it to the point that it becomes sticky. Mix in the macadamia nuts.

9. Spread the Vanilla Pudding into the prepared shell. Spoon the Pineapple Filling evenly over the pudding. Cover with the streusel. Bake at 350°F. for 25 minutes, or until the top is golden brown and the filling is just bubbling. Transfer to a rack to cool, then refrigerate to set for 30 minutes. Serve slightly cooled or at room temperature.

cranberry-walnut PIE

It is always a surprise to find that cranberries, native to New England, and grown primarily on Cape Cod and in southern New Jersey, are popular all over the world. Native Americans found their tart flavor to be a perfect accompaniment to meat but, because no natural sweeteners were available, cranberries were never used in desserts. Once cane sugar became readily available in the nineteenth century, sweetened cranberry recipes became more and more popular. In the 1970s and 1980s, cranberry desserts reached the height of sophistication as America turned into the gourmet food capital of the world. This pie is dense and fruity, like a mince pie, but the tangy cranberries give it quite a punch.

MAKES ONE 9-INCH PIE OR 9½-INCH TART

CRANBERRY-WALNUT FILLING

¾ cup orange juice

1 teaspoon vanilla extract

¼ cup cornstarch

Grated zest of one orange (about 2 tablespoons zest)

One 12-ounce bag of fresh or frozen cranberries

2 tablespoons unsalted butter

1 cup granulated sugar

½ cup coarsely chopped walnuts

½ cup golden raisins

1 Granny Smith apple, peeled, cored and cut into ½-inch chunks
   (about ¾ cup)

1 single-crust Basic Pie Shell (page 19) or Basic Tart Shell (page 20),
   blind baked (see page 15)
Whipped Cream (page 250), for garnish

1. Preheat the oven to 350°F., arranging a rack in the middle position.

2. In a small bowl, whisk together ¼ cup of the orange juice, the vanilla and cornstarch. Let rest for 1 minute, whisk again and set aside.

3. In a medium saucepan, cook the remaining ½ cup of orange juice, the zest, cranberries, butter and sugar over medium heat until the mixture is bubbly, about 7 minutes. Remove from heat and stir in the walnuts, raisins and apple chunks, then stir in the cornstarch mixture.

4. Pour the filling into the prepared shell and bake at 350°F. for 20 minutes, or until bubbly and set. Transfer to a rack to cool.

5. Serve topped with Whipped Cream.

So just what is the difference between a pie and a tart? In a word (or two), it's tender versus crisp. Because they are made with such a tender, flaky dough, pies must be baked in and served out of pie pans whose sloped sides support the delicate crust. If it is turned out of the pan, the pie might collapse.

Tarts are made with a crisp dough that is sturdy enough to stand on its own. They are baked in a tart ring with a removable bottom so the pastry can easily be released from the pan for serving. Some tart doughs are as stiff as a cookie. Our tart crust is nice and flaky but still sturdy enough to stand alone.

pecan PIE

Mississippi, Alabama, Georgia and Texas all claim to be the birthplace of pecan pie. I think it's a moot point. When something tastes as good as crisp pecans baked in sweet "clear custard," who cares where it came from? And this is the best pecan pie recipe you'll ever taste. Quite a boast for a Yankee to make, but I stand by my claim.

Because clear custard fillings are so rich and sweet and gooey, crisp tart shells are the perfect foil and, I believe, make a better container for this pie.

MAKES ONE 9-INCH PIE OR 9½-INCH TART

CLEAR CUSTARD

¾ cup granulated sugar

4 large eggs

1 cup dark corn syrup

2 tablespoons dark rum

1 tablespoon vanilla extract

4 tablespoons unsalted butter, melted

2 cups pecan halves

1 Basic Tart Shell (page 20) or single-crust Basic Pie Shell (page 19),
   blind baked (see page 15)

1. Preheat the oven to 350°F., arranging a rack in the middle position.

2. Make the Clear Custard: In a large bowl, lightly beat together the sugar, eggs, corn syrup, rum and vanilla, just enough to blend. Mix in the melted butter.

3. Place the tart shell, still in its ring, on a rimmed cookie sheet to catch any drips. Spread the pecans in the prepared shell and cover with the custard, making sure that all of the nuts are coated. Bake at 350°F. for 30 minutes, or until tiny bubbles appear around the edges and the center looks barely set. Set the tart (yes, still on that cookie sheet) on a rack to cool down.

4. Serve straight up . . . or with a whipped-cream chaser. Or if you're feeling particularly decadent, try it with Chocolate Truffle Drizzle (recipe follows).

CHOCOLATE TRUFFLE DRIZZLE FOR PECAN PIE

Pecan pies are very sweet to start with so a semisweet drizzle might take them right over the top. If that's what you like, then go for it. Personally, I prefer a bittersweet chocolate drizzle that contrasts with the sweetness of the filling.

2 ounces bittersweet or semisweet chocolate, coarsely chopped
¼ cup heavy or whipping cream
1 teaspoon instant espresso powder
1 tablespoon bourbon (optional)

1. Put the chocolate in a small bowl. In a small saucepan, stir together the cream, instant espresso and bourbon, if using. Set over medium heat and when the mixture just barely starts to boil, pour the hot cream mixture over the chocolate. Working from the center out, gently stir with a whisk to melt and blend. Continue stirring until smooth.

2. Let sit for 15 minutes to thicken, then, with a slotted spoon, drizzle over your baked Pecan Pie. Refrigerate to set for 30 minutes.

VARIATIONS

CASHEW PIE Substitute 2 cups roasted, unsalted cashews for the pecans.

MACADAMIA PIE Substitute 2 cups roasted, unsalted and coarsely chopped macadamias for the pecans.

HAZELNUT PIE Substitute 2 cups roasted, skinned hazelnuts for the pecans and 3 tablespoons hazelnut liqueur, such as Frangelico, for the vanilla and rum.

> Unlike their milky cousins, clear custards are made with a mixture of eggs and sugar syrup. The most famous clear custard pies are Pecan, Shoofly (page 44) and Maple-Walnut (page 42). Because of their high sugar content, these sticky, gooey pie fillings have excellent keeping qualities.

MAPLE-WALNUT pie

From eastern Canada to New England, the combination of long cold nights and sunny days in late winter really gets that maple sap flowing. When that sap is boiled down it makes the sweet nectar that Americans have come to love—both on their pancakes and combined with walnuts in desserts.

There are many versions of maple-walnut pie. Some versions even contain cider vinegar or lemon. In Maine and parts of Canada they are often made with a sticky clear filling, like the clear custard in a pecan pie. Others are filled with milk custards that wiggle and jiggle. Our pie lies right in between: a perfectly sweet and silky ending for a cool-weather brunch, lunch or dinner. Just make sure that you use real maple syrup. The artificial stuff just doesn't cut the mustard.

MAKES ONE 9-INCH PIE OR 9½-INCH TART

2 cups (about 7 ounces) walnut pieces

CUSTARD
¾ cup heavy cream
1 cup pure maple syrup
½ cup lightly packed light brown sugar
4 large eggs

1 Basic Tart Shell (page 20) or single-crust Basic Pie Shell (page 19), blind baked (see page 15)

1. Preheat the oven to 300°F., arranging a rack in the middle position. Spread the walnuts on a cookie sheet and toast in the oven for 5 minutes, until fragrant. Do not let them color too much. Transfer to a rack to cool.

2. Make the Custard: In a medium, heavy-bottomed saucepan over medium heat, cook the cream and ½ cup of the maple syrup to the point where the mixture is just barely starting to boil.

3. Put the remaining ½ cup of maple syrup, the brown sugar and eggs in a large bowl and gently whisk just

BAKER'S NOTEBOOK

If you can find it, use a dark, Grade B maple syrup. It has richer flavor, making it a perfect choice for baking.

to blend. Continue whisking, and slowly drizzle in the hot cream mixture so that the eggs are warmed up gradually.

4. Spread the walnuts into the prepared shell and strain the custard over them, making sure that all of the nuts are coated. Bake at 300°F. for 25 to 30 minutes, until the custard is just set but still jiggly. Transfer to a rack to cool, then refrigerate for at least 1 hour.

5. Serve chilled.

> **Patrick Towle, a grocer from St. Paul, Minnesota, came up with the idea of blending real maple syrup with sugar syrup to make a reasonably priced pancake topping. He packed it into a tin shaped like a little log cabin in honor of his boyhood hero, Abraham Lincoln. The familiar pancake syrup was born.**

It takes more than 30 gallons of sap to make 1 gallon of syrup.

shoofly PIE

Gooey molasses filling and spicy gingerbread streusel make Shoofly Pie the superstar of Amish country. Depending on how they are put together, there are different types of shooflies. When the crumbs and molasses are assembled in alternating layers, it's called a "gravel pie" and is often eaten for breakfast. The following recipe calls for a thick layer of spicy crumbs, hovering over a sweet, viscous molasses filling. It's the inimitable "wet bottom" shoofly pie.

Now what about the name? Some say the pie was first invented as a decoy to attract flies away from the good stuff. But how could a pie as tempting as this play second fiddle to any other pastry? It's so delectable, in fact, some say it becomes a constant job to "shoo the flies away." Those flies must know what good pie is all about.

MAKES ONE 9-INCH PIE OR 9$^1/_2$-INCH TART

SPICE STREUSEL

1 cup all-purpose flour

$^1/_2$ cup lightly packed dark brown sugar

$^1/_2$ teaspoon ground cinnamon

$^1/_2$ teaspoon grated nutmeg

$^1/_4$ teaspoon ground cloves

$^1/_4$ teaspoon ground ginger

6 tablespoons unsalted butter, cut into pea-size bits

SHOOFLY FILLING

$^1/_2$ cup molasses

$^1/_2$ cup dark corn syrup

3 large eggs

1 teaspoon vanilla extract

$^1/_2$ teaspoon baking soda

1 single-crust Basic Pie Shell (page 19) or Basic Tart Shell (page 20),
blind baked (see page 15)
Whipped Cream (page 250), for garnish

1. Preheat the oven to 350°F., arranging a rack in the middle position.

2. Make the Spice Streusel: In a medium bowl, combine the flour, brown sugar, cinnamon, nutmeg, cloves and ginger. Work in the butter, rubbing and pinching it with your fingers until the mixture looks mealy and lumpy. Don't overwork it to the point that it becomes sticky. Set aside in a cool place until ready to use.

3. Make the Shoofly Filling: In a small saucepan, bring ½ cup of water to boil. In a medium bowl, mix together the molasses, corn syrup, eggs and vanilla. Stir the baking soda into the boiling water, then stir it into the molasses mixture.

4. Pour the filling into the prepared shell, filling up to ¼ inch from the top of the crust. Sprinkle on the streusel, taking care not to overfill the shell. Bake at 350°F. for 30 minutes, or until set.

5. Transfer to a rack to cool. Serve with plenty of whipped cream.

BAKER'S NOTEBOOK

Even a small leak in a clear custard tart or pie can turn out to be a sticky, disgusting bummer. The best way to prevent this is to moisten little scraps of dough and fill them into anything that looks like a crack, a hole or any other potentially leaky spot in your blind-baked shell.

VINEGAR pie

Attention: Do not turn the page. *This is a recipe that you really should try!*

When lemons were out of season, or just too expensive, millions of bakers figured out how to make a tart, "curd-style" pie filling (like the one used in lemon meringue pie) with vinegar. Cheap and always available, it turned out to be just the right stuff for adding some pucker to a pie.

Okay, this pie may sound a little . . . er, different, but don' t be deterred. It was a real favorite a hundred years ago and if there ever was a pie that is deserving of rediscovery, this scrumptious old-time favorite is it. Jerry Lewis (yes, that *Jerry Lewis) has often reminisced about the wonderful vinegar pie that his grandma used to bake. Of course Grandma Lewis didn' t know about fancy-pants balsamic vinegar, but that won' t stop us from going upscale. Try it and get ready for a newfangled flavor surprise. On its own, vinegar pie is truly amazing. Topped with fresh berries, its the eighth wonder of the world.*

MAKES ONE 9-INCH PIE OR 9½-INCH TART

2 tablespoons cornstarch

½ cup light cream

2 large eggs

4 large egg yolks

1 teaspoon vanilla extract

½ cup balsamic vinegar

¾ cup granulated sugar

4 tablespoons unsalted butter

1 single-crust Basic Pie Shell (page 19) or Basic Tart Shell (page 20), fully baked (see page 15)

1 pint of fresh strawberries, or ½ pint of fresh raspberries or blackberries, for garnish (optional)

1. In a medium bowl, whisk the cornstarch into the cream. Let rest for 1 minute, then whisk again. Whisk in the eggs, yolks and vanilla.

2. In a medium saucepan, bring the vinegar, sugar, butter, and $3/4$ cup of water to a boil over medium heat.

3. While gently whisking the egg mixture, slowly drizzle the hot vinegar mixture into it until completely incorporated. While constantly whisking and scraping the bottom of the pot, cook over medium heat until tiny bubbles boil up continuously for 10 seconds. Strain the curd into a bowl and let cool to room temperature.

4. Spread the cooled filling into the pie shell, then refrigerate for 30 minutes.

5. Decorate with berries, if you like, and serve chilled.

NOTEBOOK

BAKER'S

When shopping for vinegar, look for white balsamic. It is sweet but delicate, and will make an absolutely yummy vinegar pie. Sherry vinegar is another very good substitute.

OSGOOD or JEFFERSON DAVIS pie

Osgood and Jefferson Davis pies. What are they, you ask? With fruity, nutty flavor and soufflé-like texture, they are two very similar and very yummy pies. Both are old-time favorites that somehow fell out of favor. Depending on which side of the Mason-Dixon line you park your oven, these pies vary only slightly. Up North, walnuts and raisins go into the Osgood, named after an imaginary fellow whose name is a conjunction of "oh so good." Down South, they prefer pecans and dates in their version, named after the first, and only, president of the Confederacy, Jefferson Davis. There are many variations of these pies, with some recipes calling for cider vinegar and others calling for bourbon. Balsamic vinegar and cream sherry might have old Jeff Davis rolling in his grave, but it all tastes O . . . s' . . . good.

MAKES ONE 9-INCH PIE

1 cup coarsely chopped walnuts (for Osgood) or pecans (for Jefferson Davis)

1 cup raisins (for Osgood) or chopped dates (for Jefferson Davis)

3 tablespoons all-purpose flour

¾ cup lightly packed light brown sugar

3 large eggs, separated

4 tablespoons unsalted butter, melted

1 tablespoon balsamic vinegar

¼ cup cream sherry (for Osgood), or 2 tablespoons brandy (for Jefferson Davis) mixed with 2 tablespoons water

½ teaspoon ground cinnamon

½ teaspoon ground nutmeg

Pinch of salt

Pinch of cream of tartar

2 tablespoons granulated sugar

1 single-crust Basic Pie Shell (page 19), unbaked

1. Preheat the oven to 400°F., arranging a rack in the middle position.

2. In a medium bowl, toss the nuts and raisins (or dates) with the flour until coated. In another medium bowl, whisk together the brown sugar and egg yolks until the mixture is pale yellow and forms a ribbon that falls off the whisk when it is pulled away. Still whisking, drizzle in the butter until incorporated, then beat in the vinegar, sherry (or diluted brandy), cinnamon and nutmeg. Set aside.

3. In a clean, dry mixing bowl, whisk the egg whites with the salt and cream of tartar until creamy, foamy and barely able to hold peaks (you may, of course, use an electric mixer). Sprinkle on the sugar a little at a time, and continue to whisk until the whites are the consistency of shaving cream: slightly glossy and able to hold soft peaks.

4. Fold a third of the egg whites into the yolk mixture to lighten it. Fold in the remainder of the whites. Gently fold in the nuts and fruit mixture.

5. Spread the filling in the prepared pie shell. Bake at 400°F. for 35 minutes, or until the center springs back when lightly pressed and a cake tester inserted into the center of the filling comes out clean.

PUMPKIN PIE
with ginger-graham crust

We think of fusion cuisine as a modern culinary phenomenon but it's been an American tradition from earliest Colonial times. Right from the get-go, colonists in Jamestown and Plymouth started incorporating native ingredients in "olde" English recipes. Corn puddings are a cross between Indian corn mush and English puddings. Pumpkin pie came into existence when settlers took the mashed pumpkin of tribes like the Massasoits, added spices and sweeteners and packed it in a pastry like an English meat pie. It was then served as a breakfast item, dessert or as a side dish, in place of a vegetable.

MAKES ONE 9-INCH PIE

GINGER-GRAHAM CRUST
½ cup (1 stick) unsalted butter, melted

1¼ cups graham cracker crumbs

¼ cup granulated sugar

1 teaspoon powdered ginger

PUMPKIN FILLING
1 cup canned pumpkin

3 large eggs

¾ cup heavy or whipping cream

¾ cup lightly packed light brown sugar

1 teaspoon ground cinnamon

½ teaspoon ground nutmeg

¼ teaspoon ground cloves

¼ teaspoon ground allspice

1 teaspoon vanilla extract

Plain, bourbon or rum Whipped Cream (page 250), for garnish

Walnut halves, for garnish

1. Preheat the oven to 350ºF., arranging a rack in the middle position.

2. Make the Graham Cracker Crust: Coat a 9-inch pie plate with 1 tablespoon of the melted butter.

3. Mix the graham cracker crumbs, sugar and ginger in a medium bowl. Add the remaining melted butter and mix well. Pat the mixture evenly over the bottom and sides of the prepared pan. Refrigerate for 15 minutes, until firm.

4. Bake the pie shell at 350ºF. for 8 to 10 minutes, until dry and solid. Set on a rack to cool. Reduce the oven temperature to 325ºF.

5. Meanwhile, **make the Pumpkin Filling:** In a medium bowl, mix together the pumpkin, eggs, cream, brown sugar, cinnamon, nutmeg, cloves, allspice and vanilla.

6. Pour the filling into the shell and bake at 325ºF. for 35 to 40 minutes, until set. Transfer to a rack to cool.

7. To serve, place a dollop of whipped cream on each slice of pie and garnish with a walnut half or two.

VARIATION

You can also bake this pie in a single-crust, blind-baked (see page 15) pie shell (page 19).

BAKER'S NOTEBOOK

Of course, you may use fresh pumpkin for your pie. It will involve a lot of cooking, draining and straining. In the end, you probably won't be able to tell the difference between your hard-earned pulp and the stuff in the can.

sweet potato PIE

All across America, yams and sweet potatoes take their rightful position next to the Thanksgiving turkey, but down south they also get sweetened up and packed into a pastry shell. When they emerge from the oven they are Dixie's answer to pumpkin pie. Some folks like to top their sweet potato pie with crumbs, while others like melted marshmallows. I am still divided between a thick coating of baked meringue or a giant glob of Fluffy Marshmallow Sauce.

MAKES ONE 9-INCH PIE OR 9^1/$_2$-INCH TART

SWEET POTATO FILLING

1 pound sweet potatoes

3 large eggs

2 tablespoons honey

^{1}/$_2$ cup lightly packed dark brown sugar

^{1}/$_2$ cup heavy cream

2 tablespoons molasses

1 teaspoon vanilla extract

^{1}/$_2$ teaspoon ground cinnamon

1 single-crust Basic Pie Shell (page 19) or Basic Tart Shell
    (page 20), blind baked (see page 15)
Fluffy Marshmallow Sauce (page 249) or Italian Meringue
    (page 58)

1. Preheat the oven to 375°F., arranging a rack in the middle position.

2. Make the Sweet Potato Filling: Bake the sweet potatoes directly on the rack until tender, about 45 minutes. Remove from oven and set aside to cool. Reduce the oven temperature to 325°F.

3. When the sweet potatoes are cool enough to handle, skin them and place the pulp in a medium bowl. Mash them together with the eggs, honey, brown sugar, cream, molasses, vanilla and cinnamon.

4. Spread the filling into the prepared shell. Bake at 325°F. for 25 to 30 minutes, or until set. Transfer to a rack to cool.

5. Top with your choice of fluffy topping and serve.

VARIATION

SPICY SWEET POTATO PIE Add ½ teaspoon of árbol chile powder or cayenne to the pie filling in step 3.

BAKER'S NOTEBOOK
One pound of raw, peeled sweet potatoes or squash will yield two cups when cooked and mashed.

In 1763, a trading and selling fair was held in Delaware. The main event was the swapping of horses and other livestock, but the fair also included an exhibition of "Ladies' Work" that included the best pies, jams and cakes. It was the predecessor of so many state and county fairs to follow.

key lime tart with
COCONUT MACAROON CRUST

Only in Key West, with its unique melting-pot cuisine and nonconformist spirit, could a pie this unique be conceived. Because of the extremely hot climate, bakers came up with a pie that required very little time in the oven. Traditionally, the eggs in the filling are "cooked" only by the chemical action of the acid in the lime juice, the same process that "cooks" the shellfish in ceviche. Nowadays, because of health concerns, actually cooking the egg-based filling over heat seems like a smarter option.

Originally, the crust for Key lime pie was made with a flaky dough, but in the 1950s it began to be made with that most Yankee of ingredients, graham crackers. This cut down the baking time even further, and eliminated the sticky problem of handling dough in hot weather. Here's my vote for the next stage in the evolution of Key Lime Pie: a coconut crust, which adds a whole new dimension to this tropical treat.

MAKES ONE 9$\frac{1}{2}$-INCH TART

COCONUT MACAROON CRUST

Nonstick vegetable-oil spray

$\frac{3}{4}$ cup all-purpose flour

1 tablespoon granulated sugar

2$\frac{1}{4}$ cups unsweetened, shredded coconut

5 tablespoons cold unsalted butter, cut into pea-size bits

2 large egg whites

1 cup confectioners' sugar

1 teaspoon vanilla extract

KEY LIME FILLING

4 large egg yolks

1 14-ounce can of sweetened condensed milk

Grated zest of 2 Key limes (about 2 teaspoons zest)

$\frac{1}{2}$ cup Key lime juice (from about 6 Key limes)

Whipped Cream (page 250), for garnish

1. Make the Coconut Macaroon Crust: Lightly coat a 9½-inch tart pan with a removable bottom with nonstick vegetable-oil spray.

2. In a medium bowl, stir together the flour, sugar and ¼ cup of the coconut. Using your fingers or a pastry blender, work in the butter until the mixture looks like coarse meal. Sprinkle on 2 to 3 tablespoons of ice water as needed and blend to bring the dough together. Pat it into a disk and wrap in plastic wrap. Refrigerate for 30 minutes. Roll the dough into an 11½-inch circle and fit it into the tart tin. It should fit halfway up the sides.

3. Mix together the remaining 2 cups of coconut, the egg whites, confectioners' sugar and vanilla. Lightly press this macaroon mixture against the sides and bottom of the dough-lined tin. Refrigerate for at least 30 minutes.

4. Preheat the oven to 375°F., arranging a rack in the middle position. Bake the crust for 12 minutes, or until lightly colored and just set. Transfer to a rack to cool. Reduce the oven temperature to 325°F.

5. Make the Key Lime Filling: In a medium bowl, mix together the yolks, sweetened condensed milk, and Key lime zest and juice.

6. Pour the filling into the blind-baked shell. Bake at 325°F. for 20 minutes, or until the filling is set. Transfer to a rack to cool, then refrigerate until chilled.

7. Serve topped with plenty of whipped cream.

(RECIPE CONTINUES) ➡

Gail Borden started producing sweetened condensed milk in 1858. The luscious canned milk product immediately became a staple of American baking.

COCONUT GRAHAM CRUST

For a more traditional version of Key Lime Pie, use a graham cracker crust, or try this crust recipe for the best of both worlds.

½ cup (1 stick) unsalted butter, melted
1 cup graham cracker crumbs
¼ cup granulated sugar
½ cup unsweetened coconut flakes

Follow instructions for Ginger-Graham Crust (page 50), substituting coconut flakes for the powdered ginger.

So, what's a Key lime and how is it different? The most common variety of lime is the Persian. It is tart, flavorful and readily available all year long. Key limes are smaller and sweeter than Persians, with a gently complex flavor that makes them tangy but succulent. They are only available in winter, usually from specialty fruit markets. If Key limes are not in season, use Persians for both juice and zest. Any fresh lime juice is preferable to the bottled stuff.

CHESS pie

This is another old-school Southern pie that, unfortunately, is rarely seen today. Originally, chess pies referred to a whole category of clear custards pies, the most famous being pecan pie. Eventually it was this cornmeal custard pie that took singular claim to the moniker. Some stories say it got its name from English "Cheese" pie; others say it refers to its long keeping quality, since its high sugar content meant it could be stored in a "chest" for a long time. The cornmeal in this pie acts like a magic catalyst, transforming the bourbon filling into an ethereal custard with a texture unlike any that you have ever tried.

MAKES ONE 9-INCH PIE OR 9^1/$_2$-INCH TART

3 large eggs

2 large egg yolks

1 teaspoon vanilla extract

1 cup granulated sugar

1 cup heavy cream

^{1}/$_4$ cup fine cornmeal

2 tablespoons bourbon

^{1}/$_4$ cup (1 stick) unsalted butter

1 single-crust Basic Pie Shell (page 19) or Basic Tart Shell (page 20),
   blind baked (see page 15)

1. Preheat the oven to 325°F., arranging a rack in the middle position.

2. In a large bowl, whisk together the eggs, egg yolks, vanilla extract and ^{3}/$_4$ cup of the sugar, just enough to blend.

3. Put the cream, cornmeal, bourbon, butter and the remaining ^{1}/$_4$ cup of the sugar into a medium, heavy-bottomed saucepan. Over medium heat, whisking constantly, cook the mixture until tiny bubbles boil up continuously for 10 seconds.

4. While gently whisking the egg mixture, slowly drizzle the hot cream mixture into it until completely incorporated.

5. Spread the filling into the prepared shell. Bake at 325°F. for 35 minutes, until the custard is just set and jiggly. Transfer to a rack to cool, then refrigerate for 1 hour.

lemon meringue PIE

Tart lemon curd smothered in an airy, creamy cloud . . . what could be more refreshing? For a pie that doesn't weep little droplets on its surface and a meringue that doesn't shrink, make sure that the meringue is spread all the way to the crust all the way around.

MAKES ONE 9-INCH PIE OR 9$\frac{1}{2}$-INCH TART

LEMON CURD

$\frac{1}{4}$ cup cornstarch

$\frac{3}{4}$ cup light cream

2 large eggs

4 large egg yolks

1 teaspoon vanilla extract

Grated zest of 1 lemon (about 1 tablespoon zest)

1 cup lemon juice (from 6 or 7 lemons)

$\frac{3}{4}$ cup orange juice

$\frac{3}{4}$ cup granulated sugar

4 tablespoons unsalted butter

ITALIAN MERINGUE

$\frac{1}{2}$ cup light corn syrup

$\frac{3}{4}$ cup granulated sugar

5 large egg whites

$\frac{1}{4}$ teaspoon salt

Pinch of cream of tartar

$\frac{1}{2}$ teaspoon vanilla extract

1 single-crust Basic Pie Shell (page 19) or Basic Tart Shell (page 20),
   fully baked (see page 15)

1. Make the Lemon Curd: In a medium bowl, whisk the cornstarch into the cream. Let rest for 1 minute, then whisk again. Whisk in the eggs, yolks and vanilla. Set aside.

2. In a medium saucepan, bring the lemon zest, lemon juice, orange juice, sugar and butter just to a boil, over medium heat.

3. While gently whisking the egg mixture, slowly drizzle the hot lemon mixture into it until completely incorporated. Return the mixture to the saucepan. While constantly whisking the mixture and scraping the bottom of the pan, cook over medium heat until tiny bubbles boil up for 10 seconds. Strain into a bowl and let cool to room temperature, then refrigerate for at least 30 minutes.

4. Make the Italian Meringue: Put $1/4$ cup water, the corn syrup and sugar in a small saucepan fitted with a candy thermometer. Over high heat, bring the mixture to 246ºF. (firm-ball stage). In the completely clean and dry bowl of an electric mixer, or using a hand mixer, whisk the egg whites, salt and cream of tartar until creamy, foamy and barely able to hold very soft peaks. With the mixer running on low, carefully drizzle in the hot sugar syrup. Whisk on high until the whites are the consistency of shaving cream: slightly glossy and able to hold soft peaks. Whisk the vanilla into the meringue until incorporated, about 4 seconds.

5. Spread the lemon curd into the prepared shell. Spread the meringue on top, making sure that it touches the crust all around. With the back of a spoon or a spatula, pull up whisps of meringue as you go.

6. Now, pick one of the following methods to lightly (but unevenly) brown the top:
Set the pie under a hot broiler for 20 seconds.
Bake in a 400ºF. oven for 4 to 5 minutes.
Pass the flame of a propane torch over it.

VARIATIONS

There's more than one way to squeeze a lemon and there are plenty of other fruits to squeeze into a meringue pie. Here are some unique and scrumptious variations, using other citrus or tropical fruits for the curd. Follow the instructions for lemon curd with the following changes:

ORANGE OR TANGERINE MERINGUE PIE Substitute 2 cups of fresh orange or tangerine juice and 1 tablespoon of finely grated orange or tangerine zest for the lemon and orange juices and lemon zest. Decrease the cream to $1/2$ cup and the sugar to $1/2$ cup.

LICHEE, GUAVA OR MANGO MERINGUE PIE Substitute 2 cups of fresh, frozen or canned lichee, guava, or mango juice for the lemon and orange juices. Decrease the cream to $1/2$ cup and the sugar to $1/2$ cup. Omit the zest.

VANILLA MALTED custard pie

All across America, creamy, smooth custard pies are a welcome sight on any table. The Pennsylvania Dutch make a cornstarch-thickened cinnamon custard for their Schlopp pie. In Virginia, the brown sugar and nutmeg-flavored Tyler pudding pie is dedicated to native son and tenth president of the United States, John Tyler. Custard pies can be made with buttermilk, evaporated milk or sweetened condensed milk—the variations seem endless. Our version is particularly creamy, with a silky texture more reminiscent of crème brûlée than anything else.

MAKES ONE 9-INCH PIE OR 9^1/$_2$-INCH TART

1 vanilla bean

1 cup milk

1 cup heavy cream

^{3}/$_4$ cup plus 1 tablespoon granulated sugar

2 large eggs

4 large egg yolks

^{1}/$_4$ cup plain malted milk powder

1 teaspoon vanilla extract

1 single-crust Basic Pie Shell (page 19) or Basic Tart Shell (page 20),
   blind baked (see page 15)

1. Preheat the oven to 300°F., arranging a rack in the middle position.

2. Split the vanilla bean lengthwise. Scrape out the seeds and place in a medium, heavy-bottomed saucepan along with the split vanilla bean, milk, cream and 1 tablespoon of sugar. Cook over medium heat to the point where the mixture just barely starts to boil.

3. Meanwhile, put the eggs, egg yolks, malted milk powder, vanilla and remaining ^{3}/$_4$ cup sugar in a large bowl. Whisk just enough to blend.

4. While gently whisking the egg mixture, slowly drizzle the hot cream mixture into it so the eggs warm up gradually. Strain the filling into the prepared shell. Bake at 300°F. for 35 minutes, or until the custard is just set and jiggly. Transfer to a rack to cool, then refrigerate for 1 hour.

NOTEBOOK

Now for the adventurous: There is a wonderful version of this pie called "slipped custard," which takes a bit of dexterity (or even sleight of hand) to make. The custard is baked in a well-buttered pie pan, then slipped out of the pan into a fully baked pie crust. The crust stays extra crisp this way.

The American dairy industry was born in 1611 when Sir Thomas Dale, the Colonial administrator of Jamestown, brought in hogs and cattle. The local Indians were quite impressed with the flavor of the cows' milk but, being used to fresh game, thought the meat was kind of bland. Today, more than 2,000,000 cows are milked every day in Wisconsin alone.

coconut custard PIE

Coconut, brought in from the Caribbean, has been a popular ingredient in Southern cooking for quite some time. The first American-grown coconut can be traced back to 1879, when the SS Providence *was shipwrecked off the Florida coast. Its cargo of coconuts floated ashore, took root and started growing in the tropical soil.*

This pie is the pure essence of coconut, with creamy custard on the bottom, crisp shredded coconut on top. Toasting the coconut intensifies the flavor. Avoid the over-processed, prepackaged, sweetened coconut sold in supermarkets. Instead, look for unsweetened coconut in health food stores and Asian markets. It has a pure, unadulterated flavor that's identical to fresh coconut, but it's a lot easier to use.

MAKES ONE 9-INCH PIE OR 9$^1/_2$-INCH TART

1 cup milk

$^3/_4$ cup heavy cream

1 cup canned unsweetened coconut cream (such as Coco López brand)

1 cup granulated sugar

2 large eggs

4 large egg yolks

3 tablespoons dark rum

1 single-crust Basic Pie Shell (page 19) or Basic Tart Shell (page 20),
    blind baked (see page 15)

1 cup shredded, unsweetened coconut, lightly toasted

1. Preheat the oven to 300°F., arranging a rack in the middle position.

2. In a medium, heavy-bottomed saucepan, cook the milk, cream, coconut cream and $^1/_4$ cup of the sugar over medium heat to the point where the mixture just barely starts to boil.

3. Meanwhile, put the remaining $^3/_4$ cup of sugar, the eggs, egg yolks and dark rum in a large bowl and whisk just enough to blend.

4. While gently whisking the egg mixture, slowly drizzle the hot cream mixture into it so the eggs warm up gradually. Strain the filling into the prepared shell.

5. Bake at 300°F. for 35 minutes, or until the custard is set and jiggly. Transfer to a rack and carefully sprinkle on the toasted coconut. Transfer to a rack to cool, then refrigerate for at least 1 hour. Serve chilled.

VARIATIONS

MANGO-COCONUT CUSTARD PIE

Fresh mango adds a refreshing tropical breeze to this down-home pie. Pick mangos that yield slightly when squeezed and are more red or yellow than green. Some dark speckles are actually a sign of ripeness.

Whipped Cream (page 250)
One Coconut Custard Pie, chilled (recipe precedes)
1 ripe mango, peeled, pitted and cut into ½-inch cubes (see Baker's Notebook)

1. Pipe or spread whipped cream around the inner circumference of the pie. Cover the surface of the pie with the cubes of mango.

2. Serve chilled.

BAKER'S NOTEBOOK

Here's an easy and orderly way to peel and slice a mango: Hold the mango flat in the palm of one hand. With a vegetable peeler or paring knife, remove the skin from the top flat side. In one large piece, slice the flesh away from the pit. (It's shaped like a parakeet's cuttle bone.) Avoid the tough "hair" that clings to the pit. Flip the mango over and repeat the procedure on the other side. A sliver of flesh may remain on the narrow sides of the pit. Slice this away.

PAPAYA-COCONUT CUSTARD PIE Substitute a peeled, seeded papaya for the mango.

lemon chiffon PIE

In the early part of the twentieth century, light-as-air sissy pies, fairy tarts and gelatin snows were quite the rage. They eventually evolved into that ethereal mousse-in-a-crust, the chiffon pie. They can be flavored with everything from fruit to nuts and liqueurs. They can also be packed into a variety of crusts, from crumb to flaky.

MAKES ONE 9-INCH PIE OR 9½-INCH TART

2 envelopes unflavored gelatin (5 teaspoons)

¾ cup orange juice

1 cup heavy cream

½ teaspoon vanilla extract

Grated zest of 3 lemons (about 3 tablespoons zest)

1 cup lemon juice (from 6 or 7 lemons)

3 large egg whites

1 cup granulated sugar

1 single-crust Basic Pie Shell (page 19) or Basic Tart Shell (page 20),
   fully baked (see page 15)

1. In a small bowl, "soften" the gelatin by stirring it into the orange juice. Set aside.

2. Whip the cream and vanilla to soft peaks and refrigerate until ready to use.

3. Set the bowl of gelatin and orange juice over a pan of simmering water until the gelatin is completely melted. Remove from the heat and mix in the lemon zest and juice. Refrigerate until slightly thickened, about 8 minutes.

4. Put the egg whites and sugar into an immaculately clean, dry mixing bowl. Set over a pan of slowly boiling water and whisk by hand for 3 or 4 minutes, until very hot to the touch (160°F.). Remove the bowl from the heat and continue to whisk (you can now switch to an electric mixer) until the egg whites hold soft peaks and are the consistency of shaving cream.

5. Fold the lemon-gelatin mixture into the egg whites, then fold in the whipped cream. Spread the mousse into the pie shell. Refrigerate for at least 2 hours to set.

left: Blueberry Crumb Pie *(page 28)*.
below: Vinegar Pie *(page 46)*.

right: Lemon Chiffon Pie *(page 64)*.
below: Banana Cream Pie *(page 68)*.
bottom: Pineapple Pie with Macadamia
Crumb Topping *(page 36)*.

 Cherry Pie *(page 26)*.

 Key Lime Tart with
Coconut Macaroon Crust
(page 54).

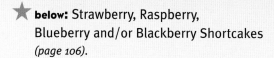
★ **below:** Strawberry, Raspberry, Blueberry and/or Blackberry Shortcakes *(page 106)*.

★ **opposite:** Sour Cherry Brown Betty *(page 104)*.

★ Blackberry-Rhubarb Crisp *(page 86).*

Apple-Raspberry Cobbler with Pecan Biscuits *(page 90)*.

ORANGE CHIFFON PIE Substitute the grated zest of 2 oranges for the lemon zest and 1½ cups thawed, frozen orange juice concentrate for the lemon juice.

COFFEE CHIFFON PIE Substitute 2½ cups of espresso or very strong coffee for the orange and lemon juice. Omit the lemon zest.

PEACH CHIFFON PIE Substitute 2½ cups puréed fresh or thawed frozen peaches for the orange and lemon juice. Omit the lemon zest.

STRAWBERRY CHIFFON PIE Substitute 2½ cups puréed fresh or thawed frozen strawberries for the orange and lemon juice. Omit the lemon zest.

VANILLA LEMON CHIFFON PIE Spread a ¼-inch layer of Vanilla Pudding (page 36) into the tart shell before filling with the mousse.

BAKER'S NOTEBOOK

If you have a source for purchasing fresh lemon juice, go ahead and buy the stuff. If you don't, then start squeezing. Whatever you do, don't use the bottled stuff. And although fresh orange juice is preferable, premium-quality juice from your grocer's refrigerated section will do just fine.

EGGNOG chiffon pie

Eggnog has generally been considered a holiday-time favorite, but this pie might change all that. It is so light and cool that eggnog could turn into a year-round treat.

MAKES ONE 9-INCH PIE OR 9½-INCH TART

2 envelopes unflavored gelatin (5 teaspoons)
1 cup cream sherry, such as Harvey's or Dry Sack
1 cup heavy cream
1 tablespoon ground nutmeg
4 large egg whites
1 cup granulated sugar
Pinch of salt
Pinch of cream of tartar

1 single-crust Basic Pie Shell (page 19) or Basic Tart Shell (page 20),
   fully baked (see page 15)

1. In a small bowl, "soften" the gelatin by stirring it into ½ cup of the sherry. Set aside.

2. Whip the cream and nutmeg to soft peaks and refrigerate until ready to use.

3. Set the bowl of gelatin and sherry over a pan of simmering water until the gelatin is completely melted. Remove from the heat and mix in the remaining ½ cup of sherry. Refrigerate for 10 minutes, or until slightly thickened.

4. Put the egg whites, sugar, salt and cream of tartar into an immaculately clean, dry mixing bowl. Set over a pan of simmering water and whisk by hand for 3 or 4 minutes, until very hot to the touch (160°F.). Remove the bowl from the heat and continue to whisk (you can now switch to an electric mixer) until the egg whites hold soft peaks and are the consistency of shaving cream.

5. Fold the sherry-gelatin mixture into the egg whites, then fold in the whipped cream.

6. Spread the mousse into the pie shell. Refrigerate for at least 2 hours to set.

chocolate CUSTARD PIE

Creamy, rich, and chock-full o' chocolate is certainly a great direction for a custard pie to take. This one goes all the way.

MAKES ONE 9-INCH PIE OR 9$^{1}/_{2}$-INCH TART

4 ounces semisweet chocolate

1 cup milk

1 cup heavy or whipping cream

$^{1}/_{4}$ cup plus 1 tablespoon granulated sugar

2 large eggs

4 large egg yolks

1 single-crust Basic Pie Shell (page 19) or Basic Tart Shell (page 20),
   blind baked (see page 15)

1. Set a rack in the middle of the oven and preheat to 300°F.

2. Melt the chocolate in a completely dry bowl or double boiler set over barely simmering water. When melted, set aside in a warm place.

3. Put the milk, cream and 1 tablespoon of sugar in a medium, heavy-bottomed saucepan and cook over medium heat to the point where the mixture just barely starts to boil.

4. Meanwhile, put the eggs, egg yolks and remaining $^{1}/_{4}$ cup of sugar in a large bowl. Whisk just enough to blend.

5. While gently whisking the egg mixture, slowly drizzle the hot cream mixture into it so the eggs warm up gradually. Strain into the melted chocolate, whisking to incorporate. Pour the filling into the prepared shell. Bake at 300°F. for 35 minutes, or until the custard is just set and jiggly. Transfer to a rack to cool, then refrigerate for 1 hour.

BANANA CREAM pie

*Bananas are as versatile as a fruit can get. They go with just about anything, from choco-
late to peanut butter. They are delicious in everything from cakes to puddings. But one of
the best places for a bunch of bananas is between layers of pastry cream in a banana cream
pie. Try rum pudding for your filling or, for a more classic version of the pie, substitute
Vanilla Pudding (page 36).*

MAKES ONE 9-INCH PIE OR 9$\frac{1}{2}$-INCH TART

RUM PUDDING
$\frac{1}{4}$ cup cornstarch
2 cups milk
$\frac{1}{2}$ cup plus 2 tablespoons granulated sugar
4 large egg yolks
2 tablespoons dark rum
2 tablespoons unsalted butter

1 single-crust **Basic Pie Shell (page 19)** or **Basic Tart Shell (page 20)**,
    fully baked (see page 15)
2 to 2$\frac{1}{2}$ ripe bananas, peeled and sliced $\frac{1}{4}$ inch thick
Whipped Cream (page 250)

1. Make the Rum Filling: In a medium bowl, whisk the cornstarch into $\frac{1}{2}$ cup of the milk.
Whisk in $\frac{1}{2}$ cup of the sugar and the egg yolks.

2. In a medium saucepan over medium heat, cook the remaining 2 tablespoons of sugar,
the rum and the remaining 1$\frac{1}{2}$ cups of milk to the point where the liquid just barely starts
to boil.

3. While gently and constantly whisking the egg mixture, slowly drizzle in the hot liquid.
While constantly whisking the mixture and scraping the bottom of the pot, cook over
medium heat until tiny bubbles boil up for 10 seconds. Stir in the butter. Strain into a bowl
and cover the surface with parchment or waxed paper. Set aside to cool down, then
refrigerate for 45 minutes.

4. Spread half of the pudding onto the pie shell. Layer on the bananas, then cover them with the rest of the pudding. Refrigerate for 45 minutes, then pipe or spoon the whipped cream on top.

VARIATIONS

COCONUT-BANANA CREAM PIE
Sprinkle the top with ½ cup toasted, unsweetened, shredded coconut (see page 10).

CHOCOLATE-BANANA CREAM PIE
Substitute Chocolate Pudding (page 77) for the Rum Pudding. Top with Cocoa Whipped Cream (page 250).

BLACK BOTTOM BANANA CREAM PIE
Use Chocolate Shell (page 72) for the crust. Fill with Chocolate Pudding (page 77).

STRAWBERRY, RASPBERRY, BLACKBERRY OR MANGO CREAM PIE
Just substitute either 1 pint sliced strawberries, 1 pint whole raspberries, 1 pint whole blackberries or 2 mangos cut into cubes (see page 63 for tips on peeling) for the bananas.

BAKER'S NOTEBOOK

Go on a safari to an Asian market and try some of the wild and exotic fruits like jackfruit, lichee, longan or macapuno (also called coconut sport). If you use canned fruit, rinse the fruit in cold water and thoroughly drain before adding to your pie. This will help to remove the "tinny" taste.

applesauce PIE

In the old days, applesauce pies, or Marlborough pies, as they were more commonly called, were made when fresh apples were out of season. Bakers could reach for a jar of home-made (or store-bought) applesauce and make a pie that was just about as satisfying as a fresh one. Smooth and comforting, this applesauce pie is a lot like a pumpkin pie that packs a powerful punch of apple flavor.

MAKES ONE 9-INCH PIE OR 9^1/$_2$-INCH TART

1^1/$_2$ cups applesauce

^{1}/$_4$ cup granulated sugar

2 large eggs

1 large egg yolk

^{1}/$_2$ cup evaporated milk or light cream

^{1}/$_2$ cup thawed apple juice concentrate

^{1}/$_2$ teaspoon ground cinnamon

^{1}/$_2$ teaspoon ground nutmeg

1 single-crust Basic Pie Shell (page 19) or Basic Tart Shell (page 20),
   blind baked (see page 15) or 1 blind-baked Cheddar Cheese Pie Shell
   (recipe follows)

1. Preheat the oven to 350°F., arranging a rack in the middle position.

2. In a large bowl, mix together the applesauce, sugar, eggs, egg yolks, evaporated milk, apple juice concentrate, cinnamon and nutmeg, then transfer to the prepared pie shell. Bake at 350°F. for 30 minutes, or until tiny bubbles appear around the edges and the center looks barely set. Transfer the pie to a rack to cool.

NOTEBOOK

BAKER'S
Frozen apple juice concentrate is a great sweetener, and it delivers a wallop of apple flavor.

CHEDDAR CHEESE PIE SHELL

Until fairly recently, apple pies were often eaten with a slice of sharp Cheddar cheese. So for a pie with an extra-sharp twist, give this cheesy crust a try.

¼ cup plus 2 tablespoons solid vegetable shortening
½ cup (1 stick) cold, unsalted butter, cut into pea-size bits
1½ cups all-purpose flour
½ cup grated extra-sharp Cheddar cheese

1. Between 2 sheets of waxed paper, spread the shortening out ⅛ inch thick. Remove the top sheet of waxed paper, and with a butter knife, score the shortening in a crisscross pattern to make ½-inch squares. Freeze for at least 30 minutes to harden.

2. In a large bowl, using a mixer, pastry blender or your fingertips, work the butter into the flour until lumpy. Add the shortening squares and work in until the mixture looks like coarse meal. Mix in the Cheddar. Gradually sprinkle on and work in a total of about 2 tablespoons of ice water until the dough comes together in a ball. Pat the dough into a ¾-inch-thick disk. Wrap in plastic and refrigerate for at least 2 hours, or overnight.

3. On a lightly floured surface, roll the dough into a 12-inch circle about ⅛ inch thick. Fit the dough into a 9-inch pie pan. Turn the edges of the dough under itself and crimp the edges (see page 16). Blind bake the shell (see page 15).

CLASSIC mississippi mud pie

Easy to make and fun to eat, gooey mud pie is a chocolate lover's dream come true. Traditional mud pies are strong in the flavor department but look like a four-year-old's handiwork that's been left to dry out in the sun. Not this mud pie. It is baked in a crisp chocolate shell that gives it a nice, neat, "tucked-in" look. But be warned: This confection is so chocolaty good that it can be deadly, so serve it with a nice dollop of whipped cream or a scoop of vanilla ice cream . . . just to make it a little less dangerous.

MAKES ONE 9-INCH PIE

CHOCOLATE SHELL

1½ cups all-purpose flour

¼ cup granulated sugar

2 tablespoons unsweetened, Dutch-processed cocoa powder

½ cup (1 stick) unsalted butter, at room temperature

1 large egg

MUD PIE FILLING

½ cup (1 stick) unsalted butter

6 ounces bittersweet or semisweet chocolate

2 teaspoons instant espresso powder

2 tablespoons sour cream

1 cup granulated sugar

3 large eggs

3 tablespoons light corn syrup

½ teaspoon vanilla extract

Whipped Cream (page 250), Cocoa Whipped Cream (page 250) or ice cream,
    for garnish

1. Make the Chocolate Shell: In a food processor or the bowl of an electric mixer, combine the flour, sugar and cocoa. While pulsing or on low speed, add the butter, then the egg. Process or beat until the dough is mixed and massed together.

2. Shape the dough into a disk and place between 2 large sheets of waxed paper. Roll into a 12-inch circle about $1/8$ inch thick. Peel off the top sheet and invert the dough into a 9-inch pie pan or $9^1/2$-inch tart ring. Peel off the remaining waxed paper. Fit the dough into place and fold the overhanging dough under itself. If using a pie pan, use a fork to crimp the edge of the dough against the rim. If using a tart ring, press the edge against the sides with your fingers. Freeze for 30 minutes.

3. Preheat the oven to 350°F., arranging a rack in the middle position.

4. Make the Mud Pie Filling: Melt the butter and chocolate in a completely dry bowl or double boiler set over barely simmering water. Set aside.

5. In a large bowl, mix the instant espresso into the sour cream until dissolved. Beat in the sugar, eggs, corn syrup and vanilla extract. Fold in the melted chocolate mixture. Spread the filling into the shell.

6. Bake at 350°F. for 35 to 40 minutes, until the filling is puffed up, cracked and crusty, but still jiggly inside. Set the mud pie on a rack to cool down. It will sink down a bit but that's okay, just fill the center with a big glob of whipped cream, or serve with a scoop of ice cream.

BAKER'S NOTEBOOK

You can, of course, bake this mud pie in a Chocolate Crumb Crust (page 21) or a Basic Pie Shell (page 19) or Basic Tart Shell (page 20).

RASPBERRY "queen of the mississippi" MUD PIE

With its intense chocolate flavor and ethereal texture, this old-fashioned fudge pie might just be the matriarch of today's trendy molten chocolate cakes. But as regal as the Mississippi Queen may be, in reality it is only a mud pie. It just happens to be the most fudgy, royal and sophisticated version ever. Call it overkill, but I like to stud the chocolate filling with raspberries!

MAKES ONE 9-INCH PIE OR 9½-INCH TART

8 ounces bittersweet or semisweet chocolate
½ cup (1 stick) unsalted butter
4 large eggs
1 cup granulated sugar
¼ cup plus 2 tablespoons unsweetened, Dutch-processed cocoa powder
½ pint raspberries (see Baker's Notebook)
1 single-crust Basic Pie Shell (page 19), Basic Tart Shell (page 20)
   or Chocolate Shell (page 72), unbaked
Whipped Cream (page 250), Cocoa Whipped Cream (page 250) or ice cream,
   for garnish

1. Preheat the oven to 375°F., arranging a rack in the middle position.

2. Melt the chocolate and butter in a completely dry bowl, or top of a double boiler, and set over barely simmering water. Stir until melted, then set aside in a warm place.

3. Put the eggs and sugar into a medium bowl or double boiler and set over slowly boiling water. Whisk by hand until the mixture is very hot to the touch but not scrambled (160°F.). Remove the bowl from the heat and continue to whisk (you can now switch to an electric mixer) until the mixture is thick and doubled in volume. (It will form a ribbon when drizzled from the beaters.)

4. Fold in the chocolate mixture, then sift and fold in the cocoa. Gently fold in the raspberries.

5. Pour the filling into the shell and bake at 375°F. for 30 minutes, until just set and crusty.

6. Serve warm or at room temperature with ice cream or whipped cream.

NOTEBOOK

BAKER'S

In season, fresh raspberries are preferred. If you use frozen berries, choose the unsweetened individually quick frozen (IQF) type. Do not thaw before adding them to the recipe—fold them in frozen.

Life on the Kansas frontier was austere and pies were usually not as elegant as this raspberry mud pie. When there weren't any apples available, pies were often filled with a mixture of crackers, dried currants and sorrel. The ingredients were humble, but the results were absolutely delicious.

BAKED black bottom pie

Classic black bottom pies combine chocolate and gelatin, but for me, gelatin just about ruins the texture of chocolate. So I've come up with versions that break with tradition— after all, innovation and ingenuity are what American baking is all about! Both are made with thick layers of rich and potent chocolate on the bottom and clouds of whipped cream on top. This recipe has a dense and flavorful baked chocolate filling. The next pie is filled with a thick layer of intensely chocolaty pudding. Both are delicious when served with heaps of fresh berries.

MAKES ONE 9-INCH PIE OR 9½-INCH TART

9 ounces bittersweet or semisweet chocolate, finely chopped

¼ cup hot, strongly brewed coffee

½ cup granulated sugar

¾ cup (1½ sticks) unsalted butter

3 large eggs

1 single-crust Basic Pie Shell (page 19), Basic Tart Shell (page 20)
    or Chocolate Shell (page 72), unbaked

Whipped Cream (page 250)

Chocolate curls, chocolate sprinkles or cocoa powder, for garnish

1. Preheat the oven to 375°F., arranging a rack in the middle position.

2. Put the chocolate in a completely dry bowl or in a double boiler, and set over barely simmering water. Stir until melted.

3. In a small saucepan, bring the coffee, sugar and butter to a simmer. Pour it over the chocolate and gently stir until the mixture is melted and smooth. Beat in the eggs until everything is smooth and incorporated.

4. Pour the filling into the shell and bake at 375°F. for 35 minutes, or until set. Set the pie on a rack to cool down, then refrigerate until just chilled, about 45 minutes.

5. Spoon or pipe whipped cream over the chocolate filling. Coat with chocolate curls, chocolate sprinkles or a light dusting of cocoa. Serve chilled.

chocolate pudding
BLACK BOTTOM PIE

MAKES ONE 9-INCH PIE OR 9½-INCH TART

CHOCOLATE PUDDING

4 ounces bittersweet chocolate

2 tablespoons unsalted butter

2 tablespoons cornstarch

¼ cup unsweetened, Dutch-processed cocoa powder

½ cup granulated sugar

2½ cups milk

1 large egg

2 large egg yolks

1 single-crust Basic Pie Shell (page 19), Basic Tart Shell (page 20)
   or Chocolate Shell (page 72), prebaked

Whipped Cream (page 250)

Chocolate curls, chocolate sprinkles or cocoa powder, for garnish

1. Make the Chocolate Pudding: Melt the chocolate and butter in a completely dry bowl or double boiler set over barely simmering water. Set aside.

2. In a medium bowl, whisk the cornstarch, cocoa and ¼ cup of the sugar into ½ cup of the milk, then whisk in the eggs and yolks.

3. In a medium heavy-bottomed saucepan, cook the remaining 2 cups milk with the remaining ¼ cup of sugar over medium heat, to the point where it just barely starts to boil. Whisking constantly but gently, drizzle the hot liquid into the egg mixture. Return the mixture to the saucepan and while whisking constantly and scraping the bottom of the pan, cook until tiny bubbles boil up for 3 seconds. Remove from the heat and strain into a large bowl. Thoroughly mix in the melted chocolate. Let cool and then refrigerate until chilled, about 45 minutes.

4. Spread the pudding in the pie shell.

5. Spoon or pipe whipped cream over the chocolate filling. Coat with chocolate curls, chocolate sprinkles or a light dusting of cocoa. Serve chilled.

Apple Crisp ★ Pear-Cranberry Crumble with Almond Streusel ★ Blackberry-Rhubarb Crisp ★ Apple-Cherry Cobbler with Pecan Biscuits ★ Apple-Raspberry Cobbler with Pecan Biscuits ★ Pear Cobbler with Hazelnut Biscuits ★ Nectarine-Raspberry Cobbler with Pecan Biscuits ★ Plum & Blackberry Buckle ★ Blueberry Johnnycake Buckle ★ Peach Pan Dowdy ★ Berry, Berry & More Berry Grunt or Slump ★ Sour Cherry Brown Betty ★ Strawberry, Raspberry, Blueberry and/or Blackberry Shortcakes

cobblers, buckles, pan dowdys

& ALL THEIR COUSINS

Call them what you will, these are all names for a family of homespun casseroles with dough on the top and hot, bubbly fruit on the bottom. They are gratifying, straightforward, casual and (here's the best part) they are a whole lot easier to prepare than pies. As a matter of fact, the only thing that isn't straightforward and easy about them is figuring out which is which. Very often, the names or techniques differ from family to family, but generally it's the topping that distinguishes them.

CRISPS AND CRUMBLES are deep-dish pies with a crumb topping called streusel. This topping can be as simple as flour, butter and sugar rubbed together but can also be enhanced with spices, nuts or grains.

COBBLERS are topped with biscuit dough, which, when baked, resembles the cobblestones that the dessert is named after.

PAN DOWDYS have pie crust lids on top, which, after baking, are broken up and dunked into the fruit filling.

BUCKLES are baked with a topping of cake batter, but this cake very often just doesn't stay put. It sinks, rises and buckles as it bakes . . . hence the name.

SLUMPS AND GRUNTS are topped with biscuit-dough dumplings and are cooked right on top of the stove. The fruit filling will actually "grunt" as it cooks, while the biscuits "slump" down into the filling.

BROWN BETTIES are fruit and crumb concoctions that are baked in layers.

SHORTCAKES are made with biscuits that have been split in half and doused with fresh fruit and topped with whipped cream.

TIPS

Many of the recipes contain some kind of alcohol as a flavoring. Although most of this alcohol cooks out, either in a saucepan or as you bake, traces do remain. If you would like completely booze-free recipes, substitute apple, white grape or any other fruit juice for the alcohol in your slurry.

Feel free to experiment. Switch cobbler biscuits for crisp toppings. Use a filling from a buckle as a substitute in a pan dowdy recipe. The toppings and fillings are all mix-and-match, so be creative and invent your own yummy concoctions.

★ **One of the essential components of the fruit fillings in this chapter's recipes is the slurry, or mixture of starch and liquid that binds the fruit together. To make smooth slurries, whisk once, let rest for 1 minute and whisk again. This will help to dissolve the starch thoroughly.**

★ **Since the sweetness of fruits varies, so does the amount of sugar that you will need. Sweetness can also be a matter of taste. If you want to play it safe, use a little less sugar, then taste your filling and add a little more as needed.**

★ **Here's a trick that we use in restaurants when we want to turn out a fresh-baked dessert in a hurry. Bake biscuits and cook a fruit filling up to 8 hours before serving time. Just before serving, cover the filling with the cooked biscuits, then pop everything in a preheated 325°F. oven for 10 minutes to reheat. Serve it piping hot, without any muss, fuss or bother.**

★ **All of these recipes are best if served warm, with ice cream, Whipped Cream (page 250), Lemon Buttermilk Custard Sauce (page 245) or Brown Sugar Custard Sauce (page 246).**

★ **For easier cleanups, always put a tray under the casserole as it bakes to catch the drips and splatters.**

★ **If the fruit you prefer is not in season, try frozen. Just look for IQF (individually quick frozen) and unsweetened fruit.**

APPLE crisp

Ah, apple crisp. Is there anything finer? Or, for that matter, easier? This is the ultimate comfort food. Tart, sweet apples, baked until they are all juicy and gooey . . . crisp, buttery streusel, all crunchy on top . . . What more could you ask for except, perhaps, some vanilla ice cream?

SERVES 6 TO 8

APPLE FILLING

3/4 cup thawed apple juice concentrate

1 tablespoon dark rum, preferably Jamaican

1 teaspoon vanilla extract

1 tablespoon cornstarch

1/4 cup dark brown sugar, lightly packed

3 pounds (6 large) tart baking apples, such as Granny Smith, Rome, Golden Delicious or Northern Spy, peeled, cored and cut into 3/4-inch chunks (about 8 or 9 cups)

3/4 cup raisins

CINNAMON STREUSEL

1 cup all-purpose flour

1/2 cup lightly packed light brown sugar

1 teaspoon ground cinnamon

6 tablespoons unsalted butter, cut into pea-size bits

1. Preheat the oven to 375°F., arranging a rack in the middle position.

2. Make the Apple Filling: In a large bowl, make a slurry by whisking together the apple juice concentrate, rum, vanilla and cornstarch. Let the mixture rest for 1 minute, then whisk in the brown sugar. Add the apple chunks and raisins to the slurry, toss to coat the fruit, then transfer the filling to a shallow 2 1/2-quart baking dish.

3. Make the Streusel: In a medium bowl, combine the flour, brown sugar and cinnamon. Work in the butter by rubbing and pinching it between your fingertips until the mixture looks mealy and lumpy.

4. Sprinkle the streusel over the apple filling, covering completely. Bake at 375°F. for 30 to 35 minutes, until crisp, golden brown and bubbly.

NOTEBOOK

BAKER'S

Apples range in size from teenie-weenie to gigantic. Larger apples will yield more edible fruit and require less work. For baking, the best to choose are Granny Smith, Golden Delicious, Rome or Northern Spy. Don't worry if you don't have an apple corer. Just peel the apples and cut the flesh away from the core with a knife, making sure to remove any seeds or seed "jackets." (For more apple information, see page 23.)

pear-cranberry crumble
WITH ALMOND STREUSEL

A crumble is a crisp, just like a rose is a rose. Unlike a rose, though, this crumble happens to be chock-full of almonds and oats, so it has a nutty, flaky crunch. Add the juxtaposition of mellow pears and tart cranberries and you have a perfect fall dessert.

SERVES 6 TO 8

PEAR-CRANBERRY FILLING
1 cup cranberry juice
1/2 teaspoon vanilla extract
2 tablespoons cornstarch
3/4 cup lightly packed light brown sugar
2 pounds Bartlett or Anjou pears, peeled, cored and cut into 3/4-inch chunks
or 1/2-inch wedges (about 5 cups)
1 cup fresh or frozen (unthawed) cranberries

CINNAMON STREUSEL
1 cup all-purpose flour
1/2 cup lightly packed light brown sugar
3/4 cup slivered or sliced almonds, toasted (see page 10) and cooled
1/2 cup old-fashioned oats
6 tablespoons unsalted butter, cut into pea-size bits

1. Preheat the oven to 375°F., arranging a rack in the middle position.

2. **Make the Pear-Cranberry Filling:** In a large bowl, make a slurry by whisking together the cranberry juice, vanilla and cornstarch. Let the mixture rest for 1 minute, then whisk in the brown sugar. Add the pear chunks and cranberries to the slurry, toss to coat the fruit, then transfer the filling to a shallow 2 1/2-quart baking dish.

3. Make the Cinnamon Streusel: In a medium bowl, combine the flour, brown sugar and toasted, cooled almonds. Work in the butter by rubbing and pinching it between your fingertips until the mixture looks mealy and lumpy.

4. Sprinkle the streusel on top of the filling, covering completely. Bake at 375°F. for 30 to 35 minutes, until crisp, golden brown and bubbly.

NOTEBOOK

Bartlett and Anjou pears are the best for baking. They are full of flavor and easy to work with, and they ripen easily in a fruit bowl at room temperature. Just hold them up to your nose. When they are ready, they will give you a delightful burst of pungent pear aroma. They will also have a little give when lightly squeezed. Stay away from Bosc pears—it's just too darned difficult to determine if they are ripe or, for that matter, halfway decent. Avoid Comice also; although yummy for eating out of hand, they turn to mush when cooked.

blackberry-rhubarb
CRISP

Europeans go wild for the strong, bitter flavor of anise but Americans seem to like their licorice sweet and subtle. This streusel has just enough sweet licorice flavor to convince any doubting Yankee that it is the perfect complement to tart spring rhubarb.

Rhubarb's most common partner is strawberry, but the blackberries in this crisp are certainly a pleasant change. If you can't find good blackberries, try raspberries, marion-berries or even strawberries. They will all do just as nicely.

SERVES 6 TO 8

BLACKBERRY-RHUBARB FILLING

1 bunch rhubarb, trimmed and cut into $\frac{1}{2}$-inch chunks (about $4\frac{1}{2}$ cups)

$\frac{1}{2}$ cup granulated sugar

$\frac{1}{2}$ cup orange juice

1 teaspoon vanilla extract

1 tablespoon cornstarch

$\frac{1}{2}$ pint of blackberries

ANISE STREUSEL

1 cup all-purpose flour

$\frac{1}{2}$ cup lightly packed light brown sugar

1 teaspoon ground anise

6 tablespoons unsalted butter, cut into pea-size bits

1. In a large bowl, toss the rhubarb with the sugar. Let sit for 1 hour.

2. Preheat the oven to 375°F., arranging a rack in the middle position.

3. Make the Blackberry-Rhubarb Filling: In a large bowl, make a slurry by whisking together the orange juice, vanilla and cornstarch. Let the mixture rest for 1 minute, then whisk in the liquid exuded by the rhubarb. Add the rhubarb to the slurry, toss to coat, then gently fold in the blackberries. Transfer the filling to a shallow $2\frac{1}{2}$-quart baking dish.

4. Make the Streusel: In a medium bowl, combine the flour, brown sugar and anise. Work in the butter by rubbing and pinching it between your fingertips until the mixture looks mealy and lumpy.

5. Sprinkle the streusel on top of the filling, covering completely. Bake at 375°F. for 30 to 35 minutes, until crisp, golden brown and bubbly.

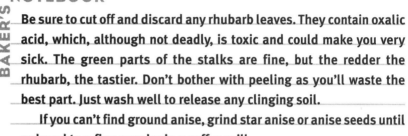

NOTEBOOK

BAKER'S

Be sure to cut off and discard any rhubarb leaves. They contain oxalic acid, which, although not deadly, is toxic and could make you very sick. The green parts of the stalks are fine, but the redder the rhubarb, the tastier. Don't bother with peeling as you'll waste the best part. Just wash well to release any clinging soil.

If you can't find ground anise, grind star anise or anise seeds until reduced to a fine powder in a coffee mill.

APPLE-CHERRY COBBLER
with pecan biscuits

Cobblers get their name from the biscuits that are baked across their tops, which look just like the old-fashioned cobblestones that used to line city streets. Here, in a twist on the classic apple cobbler, we use sweet-tart, dried Michigan cherries (which, by the way, are now available in specialty shops, health food stores, fancy markets, and even many super-markets) and nutty pecan biscuits . . . Yum!

SERVES 8

PECAN BISCUITS

2 cups cake flour

3 tablespoons granulated sugar

2 teaspoons baking powder

$3/4$ teaspoon salt

$1/2$ cup coarsely chopped pecans

$1/2$ cup (1 stick) cold butter, cut into pea-size bits

1 cup heavy cream

APPLE-CHERRY FILLING

$3/4$ cup thawed apple juice concentrate

2 tablespoons dark rum, preferably Jamaican

1 teaspoon vanilla extract

1 tablespoon cornstarch

$1/4$ cup lightly packed dark brown sugar

$3/4$ cup dried cherries

3 pounds (6 large) tart baking apples, such as Granny Smith, Rome, Golden
    Delicious or Northern Spy, peeled, cored and cut into $3/4$-inch chunks
    (about 8 or 9 cups)

Egg wash: 1 large egg white mixed with 2 tablespoons water

2 tablespoons Demerara, coarse-grain or granulated sugar, for sprinkling

1. Make the Pecan Biscuits: In a large bowl, stir together the flour, sugar, baking powder, salt and pecans. Using a pastry blender, an electric mixer with the flat beater attachment or your fingertips, work in the butter until the mixture resembles coarse meal. Mix in the cream to form a soft dough. Knead for 10 seconds, then lightly flour the dough and pat it out on a cookie sheet in a ¾-inch-thick layer. Cover with plastic wrap or waxed paper and refrigerate for at least 30 minutes, until firm.

2. Preheat the oven to 375°F., arranging a rack in the middle position.

3. Make the Apple-Cherry Filling: In a large bowl, make a slurry by whisking together the apple juice concentrate, rum, vanilla and cornstarch. Let the mixture rest for 1 minute, then whisk in the brown sugar. Add the cherries and apple chunks to the slurry, toss to coat the fruit, then transfer the filling to a shallow 2½-quart baking dish. Cover with foil and bake at 375°F. for 20 minutes.

4. Meanwhile, uncover the biscuit dough and use a round cutter to cut out 2¼-inch biscuits. Pat the scraps together and recut to make a total of 8 biscuits.

5. Take the baking dish out of the oven and remove the foil. Place the biscuits on top of the filling at ½-inch intervals. Brush the egg wash onto the biscuits, then sprinkle them with the Demerara sugar. Return to the oven and bake for 20 more minutes, until the biscuits are tanned and firm and the filling is bubbly and thickened.

> **An old Appalachian dessert was leftover biscuits from breakfast or the previous night's supper, layered with applesauce and brown sugar and baked.**

It takes 8 pounds of fresh cherries to make 1 pound of dried.

apple-raspberry cobbler
WITH PECAN BISCUITS

Apple and raspberries aren't often seen together, but after you taste how splendidly they complement each other, you will wonder why this is not a more common combination. This cobbler is a do-ahead wonder. It lends itself perfectly to the very convenient method of baking the biscuits and filling separately, so you can prepare it all ahead of time and still serve it fresh from the oven.

 SERVES 8

APPLE-RASPBERRY FILLING

³/₄ cup thawed apple juice concentrate

2 tablespoons dark rum, preferably Jamaican

1 teaspoon vanilla extract

2 tablespoons cornstarch

¹/₂ cup lightly packed dark brown sugar

3 pounds (6 large) tart baking apples, such as Granny Smith, Rome, Golden Delicious or Northern Spy, peeled, cored and cut into ³/₄-inch chunks (about 8 or 9 cups)

1 pint fresh raspberries or 2 cups frozen (unthawed) raspberries

Pecan Biscuits (page 88), assembled through step 1

Egg wash: 1 egg white mixed with 2 tablespoons water

2 tablespoons Demerara, coarse-grain or granulated sugar, for sprinkling

1. Preheat the oven to 375°F., arranging a rack in the middle position.

2. Make the Apple-Raspberry Filling: In a large bowl, make a slurry by whisking together the apple juice concentrate, rum, vanilla and cornstarch. Let the mixture rest for 1 minute, then whisk in the brown sugar. Add the apple chunks to the slurry, toss to coat the fruit, then transfer the mixture to a shallow 2¹/₂-quart baking dish.

3. Cover the dish with foil and bake at 375°F. for 20 minutes. Uncover and bake for 10 more minutes, stirring occasionally for even cooking. It is done when the apples are just tender and the filling is clear and thickened.

4. Meanwhile, uncover the biscuit dough and use a round cutter to cut out 2¼-inch biscuits. Pat the scraps together and recut to make a total of 8. Arrange them at 2-inch intervals on a nonstick or parchment-lined cookie sheet. Brush the egg wash on the biscuits, then sprinkle on the sugar. Bake at 375°F. for 20 minutes, or until tanned and springy.

5. Fold the raspberries into the baked apple mixture. Arrange the baked biscuits on top of the filling. This will keep, covered, at room temperature for up to 10 hours.

6. To serve, preheat the oven to 325°F. and bake for 8 to 10 minutes, just to heat through.

In 1930, Lively Willoughby (yes, that was someone's name), a baker in Louisville, Kentucky, devised a method of slicing and stacking unbaked biscuit dough, then wrapping it in foil and freezing it. After a few unsuccessful explosions, he perfected the method and sold it to Ballard & Ballard Flour, which was later bought by the Pillsbury Company.

PEAR COBBLER
with hazelnut biscuits

Hazelnuts have a distinct and wonderful flavor. Many people, myself included, believe them to be the veritable caviar of the nut world. They are considered quite "European" by many folks, but the Willamette Valley in Oregon produces some of the best hazelnuts in the world. Here is an elegant and sophisticated cobbler that will turn any doubter into a true hazelnut convert.

 SERVES 8

HAZELNUT BISCUITS

1³/₄ cups cake flour

3 tablespoons granulated sugar

2 teaspoons baking powder

¹/₂ teaspoon salt

¹/₂ cup skinned, roasted and coarsely chopped hazelnuts (see Baker's Notebook)

¹/₂ cup (1 stick) cold butter, cut into pea-size bits

¹/₂ cup heavy cream

¹/₄ cup hazelnut liqueur, such as Frangelico

Hazelnut egg wash: 1 large egg white mixed with 1 tablespoon hazelnut liqueur, such as Frangelico

3 tablespoons finely chopped hazelnuts

1¹/₂ tablespoons Demerara, coarse-grain or granulated sugar, for sprinkling

PEAR FILLING

3 tablespoons unsalted butter

³/₄ cup lightly packed light brown sugar

2 pounds (4) Bartlett or Anjou pears, peeled, cored and cut into eighths (about 5 cups)

¹/₂ cup sweet imported Marsala wine

¹/₂ cup heavy cream

1. Make the Hazelnut Biscuits: In a large bowl, stir together the flour, sugar, baking powder, salt and hazelnuts. Using a pastry blender, an electric mixer with the flat beater attachment or your fingertips, work in the butter until the mixture resembles coarse meal. Mix in the cream and hazelnut liqueur to form a soft dough. Knead for just 10 seconds, then lightly flour the dough and pat it out on a cookie sheet in a 1-inch-thick layer. Cover with plastic wrap or waxed paper and refrigerate for at least 1 hour and up to 8 hours.

2. Preheat the oven to 375°F., arranging a rack in the middle position.

3. Uncover the biscuit dough, and use a round cutter to cut out 2¼-inch biscuits. Pat the scraps together and recut to make a total of 8 biscuits. Arrange them at 2-inch intervals on a nonstick or parchment-lined cookie sheet. Brush a light coating of egg wash on the biscuits. Sprinkle a teaspoon of finely chopped hazelnuts and ½ teaspoon of sugar on each biscuit.

4. Bake at 375°F. for 20 minutes, or until slightly tanned and springy. Transfer the cookie sheet to a rack to cool.

5. Make the Pear Filling: In a large skillet, melt the butter over high heat. Stir in the brown sugar. Add the pears and cook and stir for 2 minutes. Carefully add the Marsala, standing away from the pan, as the mixture may start to flambé. After 2 minutes, any flames should subside. Add the cream and cook for 3 more minutes to thicken.

6. Top with the biscuits and serve immediately.

NOTEBOOK

BAKER'S

Many grocers and health food stores sell skinned and roasted hazelnuts. If you cannot find them, roast skinned hazelnuts for 10 minutes at 350°F. If you can only find hazelnuts with their skins still on, roast them for 10 minutes at 350°F., then wait 2 minutes and rub them in a coarse towel to get most of the skins off.

Use caution. Flambéed desserts can be dangerous!
- **Make sure that nothing flammable is near the pan.**
- **Never pour straight from the bottle. Measure out flammable liquids into a small pitcher.**
- **Stand back when adding alcohol to a hot pan.**

NECTARINE-RASPBERRY COBBLER with pecan biscuits

Here is a cobbler that is perfect for midsummer, when nectarines and raspberries are at their best. Since you don't have to peel the nectarines, it is a cinch to make. You can mix, roll and bake the biscuits in the morning when it's cool. I like this fruit combination with Pecan Biscuits, but you can try Hazelnut Biscuits (page 92) or the biscuits for the shortcake on page 106.

SERVES 8

3½ pounds (about 9) large, ripe nectarines

½ cup granulated sugar

Pecan Biscuits (page 88), assembled through step 1

Egg wash: 1 large egg mixed with 2 tablespoons water

2 tablespoons Demerara, coarse-grain or granulated sugar,
    for sprinkling

2 teaspoons vanilla extract

1 tablespoon cornstarch

2 tablespoons raspberry liqueur, such as framboise, or elderberry cordial
    (see Baker's Notebook)

1 pint fresh or 2 cups individually quick frozen raspberries

1. Slice the nectarines along their creases and twist them into halves. With a teaspoon, pry out the pits. Slice each nectarine half into 4 wedges. Sprinkle on the sugar and let sit for 1 hour.

2. Preheat the oven to 375°F., arranging a rack in the middle position. Use a round cutter to cut out 2¼-inch biscuits. Pat the scraps together and recut to make a total of 8. Arrange them at 2-inch intervals on a nonstick or parchment-lined cookie sheet. Brush egg wash on the biscuits, then sprinkle on the Demerara sugar. Bake at 375°F. for 20 minutes, or until tanned and springy. Transfer the cookie sheet to a rack to cool.

3. In a large saucepan, make a slurry by whisking together the juice that has exuded from the nectarines with the vanilla, cornstarch and liqueur. Whisk and cook over medium heat for 1 minute, until thickened. Remove from the heat and stir in the nectarines, then the raspberries. Transfer the filling to a shallow 2½-quart baking dish.

4. Place the biscuits on top of the filling and bake at 375°F. for 10 minutes to just heat through. Serve immediately.

VARIATION

PEACH-BLACKBERRY COBBLER Substitute 3½ pounds of ripe peaches for the nectarines. Peel them according to the instructions on page 30. Substitute 1 pint of fresh blackberries for the raspberries.

NOTEBOOK

BAKER'S Elderberry cordial is an intensely flavored, nonalcoholic beverage. It is available at specialty food stores.

plum & blackberry
BUCKLE

To call a buckle a cobbler made with cake batter is to underplay the genius of this combination. When that cake batter bakes, it sinks, buckles, soaks up all those fruit juices and creates a tutti-frutti masterpiece. You can make this without the blackberries, but do not omit the prune (or dried plum, as they're now called) juice from your slurry.

SERVES 6 TO 8

PLUM FILLING

2 pounds (about 10) black or Santa Rosa plums

1/2 cup prune juice

1 teaspoon vanilla extract

2 tablespoons cornstarch

2 tablespoons granulated sugar

1 pint blackberries

YELLOW CAKE

3/4 cup cake flour

3/4 teaspoon baking powder

1/4 teaspoon salt

3 tablespoons unsalted butter, at room temperature

1/2 cup granulated sugar

1 large egg

1/4 cup milk

1 teaspoon vanilla extract

1. Preheat the oven to 375°F., arranging a rack in the middle position.

2. Make the Plum Filling: Slice each plum in half around its crease. Twist the two halves and pull apart. With a spoon, pluck out the pit. Cut each half in two.

3. In a large bowl, make a slurry by whisking together the prune juice, vanilla and cornstarch. Let the mixture rest for 1 minute, then whisk in the sugar. Add the plums to the slurry, toss to coat, then fold in the blackberries. Transfer the filling to a shallow 2½-quart baking dish. Cover the dish with foil and bake at 375°F. for 10 minutes.

4. Make the Yellow Cake: Sift the flour, baking powder and salt together 3 times.

5. Using an electric mixer or hand mixer, beat the butter and sugar together at high speed for 15 seconds, or until combined. Add the egg and beat until the mixture is light and fluffy, about 4 more minutes.

6. With the mixer on its lowest setting, beat in a third of the flour mixture. Beat in half of the milk and all of the vanilla, then another third of the flour mixture. Beat in the remaining milk and then the remaining flour.

7. Take the plum filling out of the oven. Remove the foil and gently stir the fruit to mix. Spread the cake batter on top of the filling and bake at 375°F. for 20 more minutes, or until the cake is set and the filling is thick and bubbly.

VARIATIONS

For some real zip, zing and kerpowie, try substituting ½ cup of imported sweet Marsala for the prune juice. It doesn't have to be an expensive one, but the domestic stuff just doesn't cut the mustard. Madeira, Tokay or elderberry cordial are some other good choices.

For a buckle with a crispy top, add a streusel topping: Prepare the buckle as above, but while the fruit bakes for 10 minutes, after you've made the cake batter, in a bowl combine ½ cup all-purpose flour, ¼ cup lightly packed dark brown sugar and 3 tablespoons unsalted butter cut into bits and work together until crumbly. Top the partially baked fruit with cake batter as above, sprinkle the batter with the streusel mixture and bake as directed.

BLUEBERRY JOHNNYCAKE
buckle

Because wheat flour had to be shipped all the way from England, Colonial New Englanders quickly learned how to bake cakes with native cornmeal. Pound cakes, Simmel cakes and Nun's cake were a few popular examples, but the most famous was Rhode Island Johnnycake, made with white flint cornmeal. More like a pancake, it was originally called "journey cake" because it was often packed up to take along on trips. Versions of it were made in the Midwest and even Utah. In some circles, a buckle like this would also be called a Johnnycake, since its sweet blueberry filling is covered by a yellow cornmeal topping. Try it with Lemon Buttermilk Custard Sauce (page 245)

SERVES 6 TO 8

BLUEBERRY FILLING

3/4 cup sweet port wine

1/2 cup granulated sugar

1 teaspoon vanilla extract

1 tablespoon cornstarch

2 pints blueberries

JOHNNYCAKE

1 cup cake flour

3/4 teaspoon baking powder

1/4 teaspoon baking soda

1/4 teaspoon salt

1/3 cup fine-ground white or yellow cornmeal

6 tablespoons unsalted butter, at room temperature

3/4 cup granulated sugar

2 large eggs

1/4 cup buttermilk

1/4 cup sweet port wine

1 teaspoon vanilla extract

1. Make the Blueberry Filling: In a medium saucepan, boil ½ cup of the port wine and the sugar for 3 minutes over high heat, to cook off the alcohol.

2. In the meantime, in a small bowl, whisk together the remaining ¼ cup of port with the vanilla and cornstarch. Wait 1 minute and whisk again. Add it to the pot and cook until the mixture is clear, about 3 more minutes. Remove from the heat, stir in the blueberries and transfer to a 2½-quart baking dish.

3. Preheat the oven to 375°F., arranging a rack in the middle position.

4. Make the Johnnycake: Sift the flour, baking powder, baking soda and salt together three times. Stir in the cornmeal.

5. Using an electric mixer or hand mixer, beat the butter and sugar together at high speed for 15 seconds, or until combined. Add the eggs one at a time, beating until each is incorporated. Continue beating until the mixture is light and fluffy, about 6 more minutes.

6. With the mixer on its lowest setting, beat in half of the flour mixture. Beat in the buttermilk, port and the vanilla, then the remaining flour.

7. Spread the cake batter on top of the filling and bake at 375°F. for 30 minutes, or until the cake is set and the filling is thick and bubbly.

If you can get wild blueberries, by all means use them. Most of them grow in Maine, in the blueberry barrens of Washington and Hancock counties. The berries may be small, but they are intensely flavorful and ideal for baking.

peach PAN DOWDY

"Shoofly pie and apple pan dowdy / Make your hair stand up / And your stomach say howdy." If you have heard those evocative lyrics without the foggiest idea of what they refer to, prepare to be enlightened.

A pan dowdy is like a crisp or cobbler but with pie dough baked on top. But it doesn' t stop there. Just before serving, the dough on top is roughly cut up with a big spoon and partially dunked into the warm fruit filling below. You end up with a combination of crisp top crust and wet, tender bottom crust. It is pie, totally deconstructed. Unlike peach pie, which can be pretty tricky to perfect, this pan dowdy is dead simple to make. (To find out about that shoofly pie, just turn to page 44.)

SERVES 6 TO 8

3½ pounds (about 9) ripe peaches (see Baker's Notebook, page 31)
½ cup granulated sugar
1 teaspoon vanilla extract
½ teaspoon almond extract (optional)
2 tablespoons cornstarch
Dough for 1 single-crust Basic Pie Shell (page 19), prepared through step 2

1. Bring a large pot of water to a boil. Slice each peach around its crease and twist the halves apart. With a spoon, pry out the pits. In batches of 3 or 4, drop the peach halves into the water and boil for 2 minutes. With a slotted spoon, transfer them to a bowl of ice water. Let cool, then slip the skins off. Working over a bowl to catch the juices, slice each half into 3 wedges. Sprinkle on the sugar and set aside for 1 hour.

2. Preheat the oven to 375°F., arranging a rack in the middle position.

3. In a large bowl, make a slurry by whisking together the juice that has exuded from the peaches, the vanilla, the almond extract, if using, and cornstarch. Wait 1 minute and whisk again. Add the peaches to the slurry and toss to coat. Transfer the filling to a shallow 2½-quart baking dish.

4. Roll out the pie dough so that it will just fit into the baking dish and prick it all over with a fork. Drape the dough over the filling and bake at 375°F. for 30 minutes, or until the dough is golden brown and the filling is thick and bubbling.

5. Before serving, use a spoon to break the crust into pieces and press them partially into the filling.

VARIATION

PEACH MELBA PAN DOWDY Follow the above recipe, adding 1 pint of fresh or individually quick frozen raspberries to the peach filling in the baking dish.

Although peaches were brought to North America by the Spanish, they got to Georgia by a much different route. In the mid-nineteenth century, Georgia resident Lewis Rumph received a gift of Delaware peach buddings. After they started bearing fruit, Mrs. Rumph would nosh on peaches while she did her sewing. Soon she had a nice collection of pits and seeds in her sewing box. When her grandson Samuel told her that he wanted to plant a peach orchard, she jokingly gave him her collection of old pits. Through some accidental cross-pollination, the trees produced a new strain of great big golden peaches, which Samuel named for his wife, Elberta. Today the state of Georgia and the peach are just about synonymous.

berry, berry & more berry
GRUNT OR SLUMP

When biscuits are cooked in a stew of berries, they turn into moist dumplings. In Maine and Vermont this is called a slump, an old term for a wet, boggy place. In Massachusetts it is onomatopoetically called a grunt, describing the gurgling sound it makes as it cooks right on top of the stove.

The trick to making a good slump is to choose a heavy skillet or saucepan that has a nice, tight lid so that the dumplings simmer at a slow, steady tempo.

SERVES 6 TO 8

DUMPLINGS

1 cup all-purpose flour

1 teaspoon baking powder

1 tablespoon granulated sugar

$\frac{1}{4}$ teaspoon salt

$\frac{1}{2}$ cup milk

1 large egg

2 tablespoons unsalted butter, melted

BERRY SLUMP

1 cup white grape juice

1 tablespoon cornstarch

1 cup granulated sugar

2 pints fresh or 4 cups frozen mixed berries (raspberries, blackberries, blueberries, or other berries)

1. Make the Dumplings: In a medium bowl, stir together the flour, baking powder, sugar and salt. Make a well in the center of the flour for the milk and egg. Mix them into the flour, then mix in the melted butter. Set the dough aside.

2. Make the Slump: In a large, deep skillet or saucepan, make a slurry by whisking together the white grape juice and cornstarch. Wait 1 minute and whisk in the sugar. While still whisking, bring the mixture to a simmer over medium heat. Mix in the berries and bring back to a simmer. Reduce the heat to low.

3. Scoop the dough by rounded tablespoons and drop into the berries. The dumplings should cover about three fourths of the surface of the fruit. Cover and simmer for 12 minutes. Uncover and simmer for an additional 10 minutes, or until the dumplings are slightly firm and cooked through.

NOTEBOOK

BAKER'S

Summer is the perfect time to go berry picking, but don't eat all of them fresh off the bramble. Spread them out on cookie sheets and freeze them solid. Then measure them out into 2-cup batches, pack them in sturdy plastic bags and put them back in the freezer. When winter rolls along, you can infuse just about any dessert with the taste of summer.

In 1629, Puritans imported apple seedlings to the Massachusetts Bay Colony to start the first orchards. Soon after, they planted pears. Later honey and honeybees, which originated in Europe, were introduced. The foundations of dessert making were soon established.

SOUR CHERRY brown betty

In an 1896 edition of The Fanny Farmer Cookbook, *this dessert was referred to as "Scalloped Apples," but by 1930 it had become known as the familiar Brown Betty: baked, gooey apples held together with a little butter and crisp, sweetened crumbs. It's like a fruit version of turkey stuffing: a moist bread pudding that thinks it's a crunchy fruit crisp.*

The most famous Betty is made with apples, but you can use just about any fruit. Sour cherries add a real zing. Mixing graham cracker crumbs and Japanese panko bread crumbs gives this very special Betty a toasty, nutty flavor and an extra crunchy texture; panko can be found in Asian markets.

SERVES 6 TO 8

2 cups bread crumbs, preferably Japanese panko

½ cup graham cracker crumbs

¾ cup lightly packed light brown sugar

½ cup (1 stick) unsalted butter, melted

2 12-ounce packages frozen sour cherries, thawed and drained, juice reserved

2 tablespoons brandy

2 tablespoons cornstarch

2 tablespoons granulated sugar

Nonstick vegetable-oil spray

1. Preheat the oven to 375°F., arranging a rack in the middle position.

2. In a large bowl, mix together the bread crumbs, graham cracker crumbs and brown sugar. Mix in the butter and set the crumb mixture aside.

3. In a medium saucepan, whisk together the juice from the cherries, the brandy, cornstarch and sugar. Let rest for 1 minute and whisk again. Whisking constantly, cook the mixture over medium heat for 10 seconds, or until thick and bubbling. (The mixture should look fairly clear and gel-like.) Remove from the heat and stir in the cherries.

4. Lightly coat a 2½-quart baking dish with nonstick vegetable-oil spray. Pat a third of the crumb mixture over the bottom. Spread half of the cherry filling on top, then pat on another third of the crumbs. Spread on the remainder of the cherries and, finally, top with the rest of the crumbs, patting them down gently.

5. Bake at 375°F. for 25 to 30 minutes, until bubbly.

VARIATION

To make individual Brown Betties, follow the above instructions, but divide the crumb mixture and fruit fillings among 8 lightly greased 6-ounce ramekins. Reduce the baking time to 20 minutes. Serve out of the crocks or invert the warm betties onto plates.

NOTEBOOK

BAKER'S

If the brown sugar is lumpy, break it up between your fingers or pass it through a strainer.

Cherry juice stains clothing, fingernails, and anything else it comes in contact with, so be sure to wear rubber gloves and an apron while assembling this dessert.

strawberry, raspberry, blueberry and/or blackberry SHORTCAKES

Strawberries might be the standard-bearers, but raspberries, blueberries, blackberries and oh-so-many other berries can hold their own between the halves of a shortcake. For my money, the best way to go is to use a mixture of berries. In season, try to find huckleberries, Oregon marionberries, red or black currants or even a few tart gooseberries to throw into the mix, but always be sure to include some strawberries. When they are sprinkled with sugar (a process called maceration) they release all of the wonderful juices that make a shortcake so fabulous.

☆ **MAKES 8 SHORTCAKES**

BISCUITS

3 cups cake flour

$3/4$ cup granulated sugar

1 tablespoon baking powder

$3/4$ teaspoon salt

Grated zest of 1 lemon (about 1 tablespoon)

$3/4$ cup ($1^1/2$ sticks) unsalted butter

$1^1/4$ cups plus 2 tablespoons heavy or whipping cream

FRUIT

1 pint strawberries

$1/2$ cup granulated sugar

1 tablespoon elderberry cordial, orange liqueur or Lillet (see Baker's Notebook)

1 pint raspberries, blueberries, blackberries or more strawberries

Whipped Cream (page 250)

BAKER'S NOTEBOOK

Lillet is a fruity French apéritif. Muscovado sugar is a cane sugar varietal grown on the island of Mauritius. It has a deep and distinctive flavor, reminiscent of coffee, toffee and molasses. It is available in health food stores and specialty shops.

1. Make the Biscuits: In a large bowl, stir together the flour, $\frac{1}{4}$ cup of the sugar, the baking powder, salt and lemon zest. Using a pastry blender, an electrix mixer with a flat beater attachment or your fingertips, work in the butter until the mixture resembles coarse meal. Mix in $1\frac{1}{4}$ cups of the cream to form a soft dough. Lightly flour it and pat it out on a cookie sheet in a $1\frac{1}{4}$-inch-thick layer. Cover with plastic wrap or waxed paper and refrigerate for at least 1 hour, until firm.

2. Preheat the oven to 375°F., arranging a rack in the middle position.

3. Uncover the biscuit dough and use a round cutter to cut out $2\frac{1}{2}$-inch round biscuits. If necessary, gently pat the scraps together, rechill for 10 minutes and cut more biscuits to make a total of 8. Arrange them at 2-inch intervals on a nonstick or parchment-lined cookie sheet.

4. In a small bowl, stir together the remaining 2 tablespoons cream and the remaining $\frac{1}{2}$ cup sugar until the mixture looks like wet sand. Spoon some on top of each biscuit. Bake the biscuits at 375°F. for 20 minutes, or until the glaze is hardened and the biscuits are springy. (Some of the glaze may spread around the pan. This is a good thing. Just snack on it later.) Transfer the cookie sheet to a rack to cool.

5. While the biscuits bake, wash, hull and slice the strawberries. Toss them with the sugar and cordial or liqueur. Refrigerate for 20 minutes.

6. To serve, split the biscuits in half. Spoon the macerated strawberries and juices onto the bottom halves of the biscuits. Add the additional berries. Top with big globs of whipped cream and cover with the top halves.

VARIATIONS

FIG AND STRAWBERRY SHORTCAKES Use 1 pint of strawberries and 1 pint of ripe black figs. Trim the stems off the figs and slice them into quarters. Macerate the fruit in $\frac{1}{4}$-cup muscovado sugar (see Baker's Notebook) or dark brown sugar.

WARM APPLE-RASPBERRY SHORTCAKES Use the filling from Apple-Raspberry Cobbler (page 90).

A Tribute to German's Famous Chocolate Cake ★ Devil's Food Cake with a Surprise Ingredient ★ Best & Easiest Chocolate Cake ★ Chocolate Icebox Cake ★ New York Cheesecake ★ Carrot Cake with Cream Cheese Frosting ★ Pineapple Upside-Down Cake ★ Coconut-Banana Layer Cake ★ Applesauce Cake ★ Nectarine & Blueberry Crumb Cake ★ Peach Shortcake ★ Hazelnut Chiffon ★ Lemon Chiffon Cake ★ Gingerbread Cake ★ Orange & Almond Cake ★ Apple & Pear Skillet Cake ★ Happy Birthday Cake

cakes

& PLENTY OF FROSTING

Like so many other innovations, the prototypical American cake was a child of the industrial revolution and the brilliant American scientists who propelled it. Cakes were late bloomers in our food history, no doubt due to the lack of ovens in early Colonial kitchens. For the first settlers of the colonies, most cooking was relegated to an iron pot that dangled over the hearth. Bakers miraculously figured out how to produce pies and cobblers under these challenging conditions but delicate cakes were just a little too tricky. In 1656 Dutch settlers established the first public bakeries and began making cakes, but it wasn't until the introduction of chemical leavening agents, like baking soda and baking powder, that American cakes developed their own distinct character. Tall, luscious, moist layer cakes slathered with frosting quickly replaced the flat, dry torts and sponge cakes of Europe. If there ever was "better living through chemistry," this was it. Chemical leaveners so simplified home cake baking that it literally became "easier than pie."

TIPS

Get completely organized before you start your mixer. This means measuring and sifting dry ingredients (such as flour, baking powder or cocoa). Take butter out of the fridge well in advance so it can come up to room temperature.

★ **Line your pans with baking parchment (not waxed paper). Using the cake pan as a template, trace a circle on the parchment, then cut out with scissors. Cakes will release effortlessly and cleanup will be amazingly easy. Parchment is not necessary if you are using nonstick pans but, despite what manufacturers say, you should still spritz them with a light coating of nonstick vegetable-oil spray. Please don't butter and flour your pans. This just leaves a burned, unsightly and foul-tasting coating on your cake.**

★ **If a recipe calls for presifting the dry ingredients (such as flour, baking powder and salt) together, then do exactly that. It could mean the difference between a fluffy cake and a dense and lumpy brick. Presifting combines the dry ingredients evenly and aerates them so your cake can retain moisture. The easiest way to sift is to pass the ingredients through a large sieve. Catch them in a bowl or on a big sheet of waxed paper. Those mug-shaped gadgets with the squeezy handles or cranks are fine but I find them to be as slow as molasses.**

★ **All of the cakes in this book can be made with an electric hand mixer, but if you are serious about baking, a stand mixer should be on your wish list: It is the best tool a baker can own. The only drawback is that ingredients may cling to the sides or bottom of the bowl. Stop the motor from time to time and scrape the bowl down with a rubber spatula to ensure even mixing.**

★ **The easiest way to bake a two-layer cake is by using two pans. Let the cakes cool completely, then use a serrated knife to level the top of each and you will have two perfect layers. If you don't have two 9-inch cake pans, you may bake all of the batter in one deep pan, provided that it is tall enough to hold it; otherwise, bake the cake in a 10-inch pan. You will probably need additional baking time, so keep an eye on the cake and keep testing it for doneness (see below). You may also** store half of the batter in the refrigerator and bake it after the first layer cools enough to be removed from the pan.

★ Cake pans are made in a variety of heights. This means that the amount of batter that they hold may also vary. If it looks like your batter will fill your pan more than halfway, just leave some of it out. It is also a good policy to keep a rimmed cookie sheet under your cake to catch any spills.

★ You may store any butter-style cake batter (yellow cake, buttermilk cake, devil's food, chocolate layer) in the refrigerator for up to 2 days. Bake your cake for an additional 5 to 10 minutes to compensate for the cold batter.

★ Ovens vary in temperature and many have hot spots. Halfway through baking, give the pans a turn, front to back. Be flexible and keep an eye on the cake. Don't depend on timers exclusively. Their ding-a-ling is simply a reminder to check your cake's status.

★ There are several tests for doneness. The center of the cake should spring back when pressed lightly. A cake tester inserted in the center should come out clean. Cakes that are beginning to pull from the sides of the pan have reached their optimum expansion. Remove them from the oven or, if they are still liquid in the center, reduce the oven temperature by 25°F. and bake until set.

★ Always cool a cake completely before removing it from its pan. Chilling the cooled cake first makes trimming and slicing the layers a much easier job.

★ For easy frosting, flip the top layer over. Use the flat bottom as the top of the cake.

★ While frosting your cake, hold it together with bamboo skewers or long toothpicks to prevent the layers from shifting before the icing sets.

A TRIBUTE TO germanʼs famous chocolate cake

In 1957, a Texas homemaker sent a Dallas newspaper her recipe for an irresistibly gooey cake made with Germanʼs chocolate and frosted with caramel, coconut and pecans. It was an instant hit and remains a favorite to this day. Itʼs a pretty sophisticated cake and not as simple to make as you would think, but the results are well worth it. Hereʼs my personal "tweak" on one of the greatest chocolate cakes in the world.

MAKES ONE 9-INCH CAKE

THE CAKE

Nonstick vegetable-oil spray

6 ounces bittersweet chocolate or Germanʼs Sweet Chocolate, coarsely chopped

$\frac{1}{2}$ cup strong brewed coffee

$2\frac{1}{4}$ cups cake flour

1 teaspoon baking soda

$\frac{3}{4}$ cup ($1\frac{1}{2}$ sticks) unsalted butter, at room temperature

$1\frac{3}{4}$ cups granulated sugar

4 large eggs, separated

$1\frac{1}{2}$ teaspoons vanilla extract

1 cup buttermilk

$\frac{1}{4}$ teaspoon salt

Pinch of cream of tartar

THE FROSTING

1 12-ounce can of evaporated milk

$1\frac{1}{2}$ cups granulated sugar

1 cup (2 sticks) unsalted butter

4 large egg yolks

1 tablespoon dark rum

2 teaspoons vanilla extract

$2\frac{1}{4}$ cups unsweetened, shredded coconut, lightly toasted (see page 10)

$1\frac{1}{2}$ cups chopped pecans, lightly toasted (see page 10)

(RECIPE CONTINUES) ➡

1. Make the Cake: Preheat the oven to 350°F., arranging a rack in the middle position. Lightly coat two 9-inch cake pans with nonstick vegetable-oil spray and line the bottoms with circles of baking parchment.

2. Put the chocolate in a medium bowl. In a small saucepan, bring the coffee to a simmer, then pour it over the chocolate. Gently stir until the mixture is melted and smooth.

3. Sift the flour and baking soda together 3 times and set aside.

4. Using an electric mixer, beat the butter and 1½ cups of the sugar together at high speed for 15 seconds, or until combined. Add the egg yolks, one at a time, beating until each is incorporated. Continue beating until light and fluffy, about 5 minutes more. Beat in the melted chocolate mixture.

5. With the mixer on its lowest setting, beat in one third of the flour mixture. Beat in the vanilla and half of the buttermilk, then another third of the flour. Beat in the rest of the buttermilk and then the remaining flour.

Baker's German's Chocolate was neither developed for baking nor reflective of any Teutonic roots. John Hannon and James Baker, two residents of Dorcester, Massachusetts, began milling chocolate in the late 1700s. Their business got quite a boost when the Tea Tax and resultant Boston Tea Party convinced American colonists to jettison their tea, and hot chocolate became the thing to drink! Years later (1852, to be precise) Sam German, a teamster working for the company, came up with a method of combining chocolate and sugar in one bar. German's Chocolate was born.

And, what about that waitress on the package? Once upon a time, an Austrian prince fell head over heels for a waitress in a Viennese chocolate shop. As a token of his admiration, he had her portrait painted. When Henry Pierce, who was then the president of Baker's Chocolate, went to Europe and saw the picture, he went ga-ga for her also. He turned her silhouette into the company logo, and it's been the symbol of the company since 1880. To this day, no one knows how he ever explained any of this to his wife.

6. In another clean, dry mixing bowl, using a clean electric mixer, whisk the egg whites with the salt and cream of tartar on high speed until creamy and foamy. While still whisking, sprinkle in the remaining $\frac{1}{4}$ cup sugar and whisk until the egg whites hold very soft peaks and are the consistency of shaving cream. Fold the egg whites into the cake batter a third at a time.

7. Divide the batter between the two pans and spread evenly. Bake at 350°F. for 30 minutes, or until the center springs back when lightly pressed and a cake tester inserted in the center comes out clean. Set the pans on a rack to cool.

8. Make the Frosting: In a large saucepan, combine the evaporated milk, sugar, $\frac{3}{4}$ cup of the butter, egg yolks, rum and vanilla. Cook over medium heat, stirring constantly, for 12 minutes, or until golden. Remove from heat and let cool for 3 minutes. Vigorously stir in the remaining $\frac{1}{4}$ cup of the butter. Mix in the coconut and let cool until thick but still spreadable.

9. Turn the cakes out of the pans and trim the tops flat and even with a large serrated knife. Spread a $\frac{1}{2}$-inch layer of frosting between the layers. Frost the top and sides of the cake with the remaining frosting. Coat the sides of the cake with the chopped pecans.

devil's food CAKE
... WITH A SURPRISE INGREDIENT

Remember in chemistry class when you combined an alkaline with an acid and it turned into a bubbly mess? In baking, this chemical reaction is a very good thing. It results in leavening, or the rising of a cake. Here, baking soda provides the alkaline. Most recipes use buttermilk as the acid, but for this old-timer we employ an acid that was a favorite of nineteenth-century bakers. Tomato juice is rarely used today, even though it has the right chemical balance and a flavorful zing that complements chocolate perfectly.

MAKES ONE 9-INCH CAKE

DEVIL'S FOOD CAKE
Nonstick vegetable-oil spray

1$\frac{1}{4}$ cups cake flour

$\frac{1}{2}$ cup unsweetened, Dutch-processed cocoa powder

1 teaspoon baking soda

$\frac{1}{4}$ teaspoon baking powder

$\frac{1}{2}$ teaspoon salt

$\frac{1}{2}$ cup plus 2 tablespoons (1$\frac{1}{4}$ sticks) unsalted butter, at room temperature

1$\frac{1}{2}$ cups granulated sugar

3 large eggs

1 teaspoon vanilla extract

1 cup tomato juice

FLUFFY WHITE FROSTING
$\frac{1}{2}$ cup light corn syrup

$\frac{1}{2}$ cup granulated sugar

2 large egg whites

Pinch of salt

Pinch of cream of tartar

1 tablespoon vanilla extract

$\frac{3}{4}$ cup (1$\frac{1}{2}$ sticks) unsalted butter, at room temperature

1 cup confectioners' sugar

BAKER'S NOTEBOOK

If you still feel skeptical about using tomato juice in your chocolate cake, just substitute 1 cup of buttermilk.

1. Make the Devil's Food Cake: Preheat the oven to 350°F., arranging a rack in the middle position. Lightly coat two 9-inch round cake pans with nonstick vegetable-oil spray and line the bottoms with circles of baking parchment.

2. Sift the flour, cocoa, baking soda, baking powder and salt together 3 times.

3. Using an electric mixer, beat the butter and sugar together at high speed for 15 seconds, or until combined. Add the eggs one at a time, beating until each is incorporated. Continue beating until light and fluffy, about 5 minutes more.

4. With the mixer on its lowest setting, beat in one third of the flour mixture. Beat in the vanilla and half of the tomato juice, then another third of the flour. Beat in the rest of the tomato juice and then the remaining flour just until combined.

5. Divide the batter between the two pans and spread evenly. Bake at 350°F. for 35 minutes, or until the center springs back when lightly pressed and a cake tester inserted in the center comes out clean. Transfer the pans to a rack to cool.

6. Make the Fluffy White Frosting: Put ¼ cup water, the corn syrup and ¼ cup of the sugar in a small saucepan. Over high heat, bring to a boil and let boil for 3 full minutes. In the meantime, using an electric mixer and a completely clean and dry bowl, whisk the egg whites, salt and cream of tartar on high speed until creamy, foamy and just able to hold very soft peaks. Add the vanilla and sprinkle on the remaining ¼ cup sugar; continue to mix on slow speed. With the mixer running, carefully drizzle in the hot corn syrup mixture. Turn the mixer back up to high speed and whisk until the mixture is fluffy, firm and cooled to room temperature.

7. Using an electric mixer, beat the butter and confectioners' sugar until light and fluffy. Gently fold a third of the meringue into the butter mixture. Fold in the remainder of the meringue until completely blended.

8. Turn the cake out of the pans and trim the tops flat and level with a large serrated knife. Spread a ½-inch layer of frosting on one layer, then stack the other on top. Frost the top and sides of the cake with the remaining frosting.

BEST & EASIEST
chocolate cake

Next time you are itching for a hunk of chocolate cake, don't settle for the store-bought variety. Take the easy way out and bake this one from scratch. You will be surprised at how remarkably simple it is to make a cake this rich and full of chocolate flavor.

MAKES ONE 13 × 9-INCH SHEET CAKE

CHOCOLATE CAKE
Nonstick vegetable-oil spray

6 ounces bittersweet or semisweet chocolate, coarsely chopped

2 cups cake flour or all-purpose flour

1½ teaspoons baking powder

¼ teaspoon salt

¾ cup (1½ sticks) unsalted butter, at room temperature

1½ cups granulated sugar

4 large eggs

1 cup milk

1 teaspoon vanilla extract

CHOCOLATE FROSTING
6 ounces bittersweet or semisweet chocolate, coarsely chopped

¾ cup (1½ sticks) unsalted butter, at room temperature

½ cup confectioners' sugar

1. Make the Chocolate Cake: Preheat the oven to 350°F., arranging a rack in the middle position. Lightly coat a 13 × 9 × 2-inch baking pan with nonstick vegetable-oil spray and line the bottom with baking parchment.

2. Melt the chocolate in a completely dry bowl or double boiler set over barely simmering water, stirring occasionally.

3. Sift the flour, baking powder and salt together 2 times.

4. Using an electric mixer, beat the butter and sugar together at high speed for 15 seconds or until combined. Add the eggs, one at a time, beating until each is incorporated. Continue beating until light and fluffy, about 5 minutes more. Beat in the melted chocolate.

5. With the mixer on its lowest setting, beat in one third of the flour mixture. Beat in half of the milk and the vanilla, then another third of the flour. Beat in the rest of the milk and flour.

6. Spread the batter in the pan. Bake at 350°F. for 35 minutes, or until the center springs back when lightly pressed and a cake tester inserted in the center comes out clean. Transfer the pan to a rack to cool.

7. Make the Chocolate Frosting: Melt the chocolate in a completely dry bowl or double boiler set over barely simmering water. Take the bowl off the hot water and let cool for 5 minutes. Meanwhile, in a mixing bowl, beat the butter for 1 minute until creamy. Beat in the cooled chocolate until blended. Gradually beat in the confectioners' sugar, then continue to beat for 2 minutes, until fluffy.

8. Turn the cake out of the pan and, using a large serrated knife, trim the top flat and level. Invert it onto a serving platter (so the flat bottom is now on top). Spread the frosting on the top and sides and serve at room temperature or chilled.

VARIATIONS

CHOCOLATE MALTED FROSTING Beat ¼ cup plain malted milk powder (such as Carnation's brand) into the completed frosting.

CHOCOLATE MOCHA FROSTING Dissolve 2 tablespoons of instant espresso powder in 1 tablespoon hot water, then beat into the frosting.

BAKER'S NOTEBOOK

The batter can be divided between two 9-inch round pans and baked for 25 minutes. Turn the cakes out of the pans and trim the tops flat and level with a large serrated knife. Spread a ½-inch layer of frosting on one layer, then stack the other on top. Use the remaining frosting to frost the outside of the cake. It may also be baked in a 10-inch round pan.

chocolate ICEBOX CAKE

In the early part of the twentieth century, the home icebox was introduced and the icebox cake came fast on its heels. This chilled cake, a mixture of whipped cream and chunks of cake or cookies, was a miracle of modern convenience, easily assembled and requiring virtually no baking. If you have any cake or cookie scraps hanging around, this cool chocolate treat is the perfect way to use them.

MAKES ONE 9-INCH CAKE

Nonstick vegetable-oil spray
Devil's Food Cake (page 116), prepared steps 2 through 4
1 pint (2 cups) heavy or whipping cream, chilled
½ cup confectioners' sugar
¼ cup unsweetened cocoa powder

GANACHE FROSTING
½ cup heavy or whipping cream
4 ounces semisweet chocolate, coarsely chopped

1. Preheat the oven to 350°F., arranging a rack in the middle position. Lightly coat a 9-inch springform pan (see Baker's Notebook) and a 13 × 9-inch baking pan with nonstick vegetable-oil spray. Line the bottoms of the pans with baking parchment.

2. Spread a ½-inch layer of Devil's Food Cake batter on the bottom of the springform pan. Spread the remainder in the 13 × 9-inch baking pan. Bake at 350°F. for 15 to 20 minutes, or until the centers spring back when lightly pressed and a cake tester inserted into the centers comes out clean. Transfer the pans to a rack to cool and dry out for 3 to 4 hours or overnight. Turn the rectangular cake out of its pan and cut it into 1-inch cubes.

3. Whip the cream, confectioners' sugar and cocoa until stiff but smooth. Fold the squares of cake into the whipped cream. (Don't worry if they break up into smaller pieces.) Fill the mixture into the cake-lined springform pan. Tamp down and even off the whipped cream with a spatula to squeeze out any air spaces. Set in the freezer for 4 hours or overnight.

4. Once the cake has frozen solid, preheat the oven to 350°F. Place the cake in the oven for just 20 seconds. Release the springform ring and flip the cake onto a plate or cake board. Remove the pan bottom and peel off the circle of parchment, then invert it onto a platter. Set aside in the refrigerator.

5. Make the Ganache Frosting: Put the chocolate in a small bowl. In a small saucepan over medium heat, cook the cream, stirring occasionally, until it just barely starts to boil, then pour the hot cream over the chocolate. Working from the center out, gently stir with a whisk to melt and blend. Continue stirring until smooth. Let cool for 15 minutes.

6. Pour the ganache over the cake so it covers the top and drizzles down the sides in streaks. Refrigerate for 3 hours, or until thawed. Serve chilled.

BAKER'S NOTEBOOK

This cake is formulated for a round cake pan that is 3½ inches or 4 inches deep. If your round pan is shallower, make the cake in a 10-inch pan.

If you have any ganache left over, let it sit at room temperature for 1 hour, or until thick and spreadable. Fit into a piping bag fitted with a ½-inch star tip and pipe a decorative border around the cake.

VARIATIONS

CHOCOLATE MALTED ICEBOX CAKE Add ¼ cup plain malted milk powder to the whipped cream.

CHOCOLATE MOCHA ICEBOX CAKE Add 1 tablespoon instant espresso powder dissolved in 1 tablespoon hot water to the whipped cream.

NEW YORK cheesecake

From Lindy's in Times Square to the neighborhood diner, New York has always been cheesecake country. In my opinion, the one served for over fifty years at Junior's in Brooklyn is still the best in town. In 1950, Harry Rosen and his chief baker, Eigel Peterson, came up with a unique version. Instead of the usual graham cracker crust, they put a slab of spongecake on the bottom, and instantly the super creamy cheesecake became the trademark of their landmark restaurant.

Here is a recipe for the perfect, classic New York Cheesecake; the following pages offer a variety of toppings and bottom crusts in two yummy variations: In addition to the Classic Graham Cracker Crumb Crust, there are Nutty Graham Cracker Crumb Crust and, spanning the best of both worlds, Graham Cracker Cake Crust.

MAKES ONE 8-INCH CAKE

CLASSIC GRAHAM CRACKER CRUMB CRUST

7 tablespoons unsalted butter, melted

1 cup graham cracker crumbs

¼ cup granulated sugar

CHEESECAKE BATTER

1½ pounds cream cheese, at room temperature

6 tablespoons unsalted butter, at room temperature

1 cup granulated sugar

3 tablespoons cornstarch

1 cup sour cream

¼ cup cream sherry or sweet Marsala

2 teaspoons vanilla extract

4 large eggs

1. Make the Classic Graham Cracker Crust: Preheat the oven to 350°F., arranging a rack in the middle position. Brush an 8-inch springform pan or an 8-inch cake pan with 1 tablespoon of the melted butter. If you're using a springform pan, wrap the outside with aluminum foil.

2. Combine the graham cracker crumbs and sugar in a medium bowl. Add the remaining 6 tablespoons of melted butter and mix thoroughly. Pat the mixture evenly over the bottom of the prepared cake pan. Bake at 350°F. for 7 minutes, or until lightly colored at the edges. Transfer to a rack while you prepare the filling. Set a rack in the bottom third of the oven and reduce the oven temperature to 300°F.

3. Make the Cheesecake Batter: Put the cream cheese, butter, sugar, and cornstarch in a large mixing bowl and beat with an electric mixer at medium speed until just blended (take care not to mix too much air into the batter). Beat in the sour cream, sherry and vanilla. Add the eggs one at a time and beat until each is incorporated.

4. Pour the batter into the prepared cake pan with the graham cracker crust. Place the cake pan in a large roasting pan and pour enough hot water into the roasting pan to come about 1 inch up the sides of the cake pan. Cover the roasting pan with foil and bake at 300°F. for 1 hour. Remove the foil and bake for 15 to 30 more minutes, until very lightly tanned, slightly puffed and barely firm. Cool to room temperature right in the water bath. Remove from the bath and refrigerate overnight.

5. To release the cake, pop it into a 350°F. oven for 2 minutes. If using a springform pan, snap the catch to release the sides. For a regular pan, invert it onto a plate covered with plastic wrap or foil. Give it a shake. Voilà! Now turn it right side up onto a serving platter and peel off the foil or plastic. If you are having any trouble, run a thin knife blade around the sides of the cake to help loosen it. This cake will last for 4 days, covered, in the refrigerator.

(RECIPE CONTINUES) ➡

BAKER'S NOTEBOOK

Before you start, set your cream cheese and butter out for several hours, so they can warm up to room temperature.
   This recipe requires an 8-inch cake pan or a springform pan that is 4 inches deep. If you don't have either, you can bake your cake in a 9-inch pan.

What would become known as Philadelphia Brand Cream Cheese was invented in 1872, in New York State, by a Mr. Lawrence of the Empire Cheese Company.

VARIATIONS

NUTTY GRAHAM CRACKER CRUMB CRUST Add ½ cup lightly toasted (see page 10) chopped walnuts, pecans or hazelnuts to the Classic Graham Cracker Crumb Crust recipe before the initial baking. Try it or the following bottom for your cheesecake, then proceed with the rest of the Cheesecake recipe from step number 3.

GRAHAM CRACKER CAKE CRUST

This is a hybrid of graham cracker crust and Junior's-style spongecake bottom.

Nonstick vegetable-oil spray
½ cup cake flour
½ teaspoon baking powder
¼ teaspoon salt
¼ cup graham cracker crumbs
3 tablespoons unsalted butter, at room temperature
½ cup granulated sugar
1 large egg
¼ cup milk
2 tablespoons cream sherry, such as Dry Sack or Harvey's

1. Preheat the oven to 350°F., arranging a rack in the middle position. Lightly coat an 8-inch springform pan or an 8-inch cake pan with nonstick vegetable-oil spray. If you're using a springform pan, wrap the outside with aluminum foil.

2. Sift together the flour, baking powder and salt. Stir in the graham cracker crumbs and set aside.

3. Using an electric mixer, beat the butter and sugar together on high speed for 15 seconds, or until combined. Add the egg and beat until light and fluffy, about 3 minutes more.

4. With the mixer on its lowest setting, beat in half of the graham cracker crumb mixture. Beat in the milk and sherry, then the remaining graham cracker crumb mixture.

5. Spread the batter in the prepared pan and bake at 350°F. for 12 minutes, or until golden brown. The center should spring back when lightly pressed and a cake tester should come out clean. Transfer the cake on a rack to cool while you prepare the filling.

STRAWBERRY CHEESECAKE TOPPING

If this is a New York Cheesecake, where are the toppings? Try this and the following two toppings for a fruity taste of the Big Apple.

1 pint strawberries, washed, dried and hulled
1/2 cup strawberry or red currant jelly

Arrange the strawberries on top of the cake. In a small saucepan, bring the jelly and 1/4 cup of water to a simmer. Whisking continuously, cook over medium heat until all of the jelly has melted and blended in. Drizzle the hot glaze over the berries in a nice, thick coating.

BLUEBERRY CHEESECAKE TOPPING

1 cup port wine
2 tablespoons cornstarch
1/2 cup sugar
1/2 teaspoon vanilla extract
1 pint blueberries

In a small saucepan, whisk together the port, cornstarch and sugar. Whisking continuously, cook over medium heat for 1 minute, until thickened. Remove from the heat and stir in the vanilla and blueberries. Spread on top of the cake.

CHERRY CHEESECAKE TOPPING

1 12-ounce package frozen sour cherries, thawed and drained, juice reserved
1 tablespoon brandy
2 tablespoons granulated sugar
3 tablespoons cornstarch

In a medium saucepan, whisk together the juice from the cherries, the brandy, sugar and cornstarch. Let rest for 1 minute and whisk again. Whisking continuously, cook over medium heat until the mixture is thick and fairly clear and bubbles continuously for 10 seconds. Remove from the heat and stir in the cherries. Spread on top of the cake.

CARROT CAKE with
cream cheese frosting

There was a time when cakes made with beets and pies filled with tomatoes were as common as cupcakes. Today, carrot cake is virtually the sole survivor of this genre. Like other vegetable cakes, this carrot cake is a "good keeper" that will stay moist and flavorful longer than most others. Its robust yet mellow taste will make you wonder why all of those other vegetable cakes fell from grace.

MAKES ONE 9-INCH CAKE

CARROT CAKE

Nonstick vegetable-oil spray

1 cup cake flour

1 teaspoon baking powder

1 teaspoon baking soda

$1/2$ teaspoon salt

$3/4$ pound carrots, peeled

1 cup granulated sugar

3 large eggs

$3/4$ cup vegetable oil

$1/2$ cup unsweetened, shredded coconut

$1/2$ cup chopped, toasted walnuts (see page 10)

CREAM CHEESE FROSTING

12 ounces cream cheese, at room temperature

$3/4$ cup confectioners' sugar

1 tablespoon vanilla extract

$1/2$ cup chopped, lightly toasted walnuts (see page 10), for decoration

1. Make the Carrot Cake: Preheat the oven to 350°F., arranging a rack in the middle position. Lightly coat two 9-inch cake pans with nonstick vegetable-oil spray. Line the bottoms with circles of baking parchment.

2. Sift the flour, baking powder, baking soda and salt together 3 times.

3. Finely chop the carrots in a food processor fitted with the metal blade or grate them with a hand grater.

4. Using an electric mixer, beat the sugar and eggs together at high speed for 2 minutes, or until creamy. Continue beating, and slowly drizzle in the oil until well blended and emulsified. With the mixer on its lowest setting, beat in half of the flour mixture. Beat in the coconut and carrots, then the remaining flour and the walnuts.

5. Divide the batter between the two pans and spread evenly. Bake at 350°F. for 30 minutes, or until the center springs back when lightly pressed and a cake tester inserted in the center comes out clean. Transfer the pans to a rack to cool.

6. Make the Cream Cheese Frosting: Using an electric mixer, beat the cream cheese, confectioners' sugar and vanilla on low speed until blended, then increase the speed and beat until fluffy.

7. Turn the cakes out of the pans and trim the top of one layer with a large serrated knife so it is flat and level. Spread ½ inch of frosting on the trimmed layer and top it with the other layer, domed side up. Use the remaining frosting to frost the top and sides of the cake, then coat the sides with the walnuts.

pineapple UPSIDE-DOWN CAKE

This cake is an all-around winner, but the sticky, gooey, brown sugary pineapple is the most irresistible part. Be sure to use an ovenproof skillet without plastic or wooden handles. If you don' t have one, make the brown sugar mixture in a saucepan and pour it into a 10-inch cake pan coated with nonstick spray. Top with the pineapple chunks, cover with batter and follow the rest of the instructions, adding 5 minutes to the baking time.

MAKES ONE 10-INCH CAKE

BROWN SUGAR UPSIDE-DOWN TOPPING

1 ripe pineapple

$1/2$ cup (1 stick) unsalted butter

$1^1/4$ cups lightly packed dark brown sugar

$3/4$ cup ($3^1/2$ ounces) pecan halves

Nonstick vegetable-oil spray

YELLOW CAKE

$1^1/2$ cups cake flour

$1^1/2$ teaspoons baking powder

$1/4$ teaspoon salt

6 tablespoons unsalted butter, at room temperature

1 cup granulated sugar

2 large eggs

$1/2$ cup milk

1 teaspoon vanilla extract

1. Preheat the oven to 375°F., arranging a rack in the middle position.

2. With a big, sharp knife, cut off the top and bottom of the pineapple. Cut the center into four wedges. Slice the tough inner core from each piece. Run a paring knife under each piece to free the flesh from the skin. Cut out any "eyes" that may remain. Slice into $1/3$-inch wedges.

3. Make the Topping: Over medium heat, melt the butter in a 10-inch ovenproof skillet (the sides should be at least $1^1/2$ inches high). Add the brown sugar and cook, stirring, until the sugar is dissolved and the mixture is bubbling. Remove from the heat, sprinkle in the pecans, and then fit the pineapple pieces evenly over the surface of the skillet. Lightly coat the sides of the skillet with nonstick vegetable-oil spray.

4. Make the Yellow Cake: Sift the flour, baking powder and salt together 3 times and set aside.

5. Using an electric mixer, beat the butter and sugar together at high speed for 15 seconds, or until combined. Add the eggs, one at a time, beating until each is incorporated. Continue beating until light and fluffy, about 5 minutes more.

6. With the mixer on its lowest setting, beat in a third of the flour mixture. Beat in half of the milk and all of the vanilla, then another third of the flour mixture. Beat in the remaining milk and then the remaining flour mixture.

7. Spread the batter over the pineapple in the prepared skillet and bake at 375°F. for 30 minutes, or until the cake is golden brown, the center springs back when lightly pressed and a cake tester inserted into the center comes out clean. Transfer the skillet to a rack to cool for 1 minute.

8. Run a knife around the edge of the cake to loosen it and place a serving platter on top of the pan. Carefully flip the whole thing over so that the cake unmolds, pineapple side up. If any pineapple is stuck to the pan, scrape it off and rearrange it on top of the cake. Let cool for 15 minutes before serving.

VARIATIONS

MANGO-MACADAMIA UPSIDE-DOWN CAKE Substitute 2 ripe mangoes, peeled, pitted and cut into ½-inch slices, for the pineapple, and use macadamia nuts cut into halves and quarters for the pecans.

NOTEBOOK

BAKER'S

How to pick the perfect pineapple:
- Gently squeeze the pineapple to make sure there are no soft spots. They indicate that the fruit could be past its prime.
- Try to pick the pineapple up by one of its inner fronds. The leaf should rip right out.
- Turn the pineapple upside down and smell its bottom. The fragrance should profoundly announce that the pineapple is ripe and flavorful.

COCONUT-BANANA layer cake

Of course you can make a traditional coconut layer cake with Buttermilk Cake (page 148) or Yellow Cake (page 146), but the tropical flavor of banana cake works perfectly with the coconut frosting.

MAKES ONE 9-INCH CAKE

BANANA CAKE

Nonstick vegetable-oil spray

2 cups cake flour

1 teaspoon baking soda

$\frac{1}{4}$ teaspoon baking powder

$\frac{1}{4}$ teaspoon salt

$\frac{1}{2}$ cup plus 2 tablespoons ($1\frac{1}{4}$ sticks) unsalted butter, at room temperature

1 cup granulated sugar

2 large eggs

$2\frac{1}{2}$ large, ripe bananas

$\frac{1}{3}$ cup sour cream

2 teaspoons vanilla extract

$1\frac{1}{2}$ cups unsweetened, shredded coconut, lightly toasted (see page 10)
Fluffy White Frosting (page 116)

1. Preheat the oven to 350°F., arranging a rack in the middle position. Lightly coat two 9-inch cake pans with nonstick vegetable-oil spray and line the bottoms with baking parchment.

2. Sift the flour, baking soda, baking powder and salt together 3 times. Set aside.

3. Using an electric mixer, beat the butter and sugar together on high speed for 15 seconds, or until combined. Add the eggs, one at a time, beating until each is incorporated. Continue beating until light and fluffy, about 5 minutes more.

4. In a medium bowl, mash the bananas until soupy. Stir in the sour cream and vanilla.

5. With the mixer on its lowest setting, beat a third of the flour mixture into the butter mixture. Beat in half of the banana mixture, then another third of the flour mixture. Beat in the remaining banana mixture and then the remaining flour mixture.

6. Divide the batter between the two pans and spread evenly. Bake at 350°F. for 30 minutes, or until the center springs back when lightly pressed and a cake tester inserted in the center comes out clean.

7. Gently fold $3/4$ cup of the coconut into the Fluffy White Frosting.

8. Turn the cake out of the pans and trim the top of one layer with a large serrated knife so it is flat and even. Spread $1/2$ inch of frosting on the trimmed layer and top it with the other layer, domed side up. Frost the top and sides of the cake with the remaining frosting. Let rest for 20 minutes, then coat the outside with the remaining $3/4$ cup coconut.

VARIATION

THREE-LAYER COCONUT-BANANA CAKE Bake two thirds of the batter in one pan and one third in another. The shallow pan needs 25 minutes to bake and the deep one needs 40 minutes. Split the thicker cake into 2 layers and use the thin cake for the third. You may also bake this as one unlayered banana cake. Use a 10-inch pan and bake for 40 minutes.

applesauce CAKE

This could be called a wholesome cake, but don't let that scare you. It's absolutely delicious and it can be easily assembled with ingredients from the cupboard, which is certainly part of the charm of applesauce cakes. In Grandma's time, it was the kind of cake that got thrown together with whatever was around. If you'd like to turn this healthy pleasure into a decadent delight, top it with Brown Sugar Frosting (recipe follows), but it's strictly optional.

This cake may also be baked in a 10-inch round cake pan.

MAKES ONE 10 × 5-INCH LOAF

$^1\!/_2$ **cup thawed apple juice concentrate**

1 cup applesauce

Nonstick vegetable-oil spray

1 cup all-purpose flour

$^1\!/_4$ **cup miller's wheat bran**

$^1\!/_4$ **cup plus 2 tablespoons rolled oats, preferably old-fashioned**

$^3\!/_4$ **cup wheat germ**

1$^1\!/_2$ teaspoons baking powder

$^1\!/_4$ **teaspoon baking soda**

$^3\!/_4$ **teaspoon ground cinnamon**

$^3\!/_4$ **cup lightly packed light brown sugar**

2 large eggs

$^3\!/_4$ **cup vegetable oil**

2 tart baking apples, such as Granny Smith, Rome, Golden Delicious or Northern Spy, peeled, cored and cut into $^1\!/_2$-inch chunks

1. In a small saucepan, simmer the apple concentrate and applesauce together for 3 minutes. Set aside to cool while you continue.

2. Preheat the oven to 350°F., arranging a rack in the middle position. Lightly coat a 10 × 5-inch loaf pan with nonstick vegetable-oil spray. Line the bottom with baking parchment.

3. In a medium bowl, thoroughly stir together the flour, bran, ¼ cup of the oatmeal, the wheat germ, baking powder, baking soda and cinnamon. Set aside.

4. Using an electric mixer, beat the brown sugar and eggs together at high speed for 2 minutes, until creamy. Continue beating, and slowly drizzle in the oil and beat until well blended and emulsified. With the mixer on its lowest setting, beat in half of the flour mixture. Beat in the applesauce mixture, then the rest of the flour mixture. Stir in the apple chunks.

5. Spread the batter in the pan and sprinkle the remaining 2 tablespoons of oatmeal on top. Bake at 350°F. for 40 minutes, or until the center springs back when lightly pressed and a cake tester inserted into the center comes out clean. Transfer the pan to a rack to cool.

BROWN SUGAR FROSTING

Turn your wholesome Applesauce Cake into a decadent treat with this praline frosting.

½ **cup heavy cream**
4 **tablespoons unsalted butter**
2 **cups lightly packed light brown sugar**
1 **cup confectioners' sugar, sifted**

1. In a medium saucepan, bring the cream, butter and brown sugar to a simmer. While carefully whisking, boil for 2 minutes.

2. Remove from the heat and gradually whisk in the confectioners' sugar. Drizzle on top of the cooled cake. Let set for 10 minutes before serving.

BAKER'S NOTEBOOK

CAUTION: This frosting may splatter while cooking. Keep your hands covered and stand back from the pot.

nectarine & blueberry
CRUMB CAKE

The nectarine—what a fruit! It's like a peach that lost its fuzz and found a bright new dimension of flavor. And, since their thin skins don't toughen up when heated (like the skin of a peach does), they don't require peeling. They go perfectly with all sorts of berries and that's why I just saturate this buckle cake with blueberries and nectarines. Your nose knows how to pick a perfect nectarine. A ripe one has a little "give" when pressed and an intoxicating aroma.

MAKES ONE 13 × 9-INCH CAKE

NECTARINE-BLUEBERRY FILLING

3 large, ripe nectarines

2 tablespoons granulated sugar

1 teaspoon vanilla extract

1 pint of blueberries

STREUSEL

1 cup all-purpose flour

1/2 cup lightly packed light brown sugar

6 tablespoons (3/4 stick) unsalted butter, cut into pea-size bits

BUTTERMILK CAKE

Nonstick vegetable-oil spray

1 1/2 cups cake flour

1 teaspoon baking powder

1/4 teaspoon baking soda

1/4 teaspoon salt

1/2 cup (1 stick) unsalted butter, at room temperature

1 cup granulated sugar

2 large eggs

3/4 cup buttermilk

1 teaspoon vanilla extract

1. Make the Nectarine-Blueberry Filling: Slice the nectarines around their creases and twist them into halves. With a spoon, pry out the pits. Slice into $1/2$-inch wedges. Toss in a large bowl with the sugar and vanilla. Add the blueberries and set aside for at least 30 minutes.

2. Make the Streusel: In a medium bowl, combine the flour and brown sugar. Work in the butter, rubbing and pinching it between your fingertips until the mixture looks mealy and lumpy. Refrigerate until ready to use.

3. Make the Buttermilk Cake: Preheat the oven to 350°F., arranging a rack in the middle position. Lightly coat a 13 $\times$ 9-inch cake pan with nonstick vegetable-oil spray. Line the bottom with baking parchment.

4. Sift the flour, baking powder, baking soda and salt together 3 times.

5. Using an electric mixer, beat the butter and sugar together at high speed for 15 seconds, or until combined. Add the eggs, one at a time, beating until each is incorporated. Continue beating until light and fluffy, about 5 minutes more.

6. With the mixer on its lowest setting, beat in a third of the flour mixture. Beat in half of the buttermilk and the vanilla, then another third of the flour mixture. Beat in the rest of the buttermilk, then the remaining flour mixture.

7. Gently fold in the nectarine and blueberry filling.

8. Spread the batter into the pan. Sprinkle the streusel on top. Bake at 350°F. for 25 minutes, or until golden brown. The center should spring back when lightly pressed and a cake tester inserted in the center should come out clean. Transfer the pan to a rack to cool.

PEACH shortcake

Shortcakes made with flaky biscuits are homestyle favorites, but what about the great big, dazzling concoctions that grace the display cakes of diners from coast to coast? An undeniably authentic diner-style shortcake (like the ones I used to make when I worked a stint in New York's Big City Diner) is made with layers of hot-milk spongecake, a cake that gets both its name and its moist, tender texture from the scalded milk and butter used in its batter. Of course the classic filling is whipped cream and strawberries but, in season, juicy peaches make a luscious and refreshing change of pace.

MAKES ONE 9-INCH CAKE

HOT-MILK SPONGECAKE
Nonstick vegetable-oil spray
1½ cups cake flour
1½ teaspoons baking powder
½ teaspoon salt
¾ cup milk
3 tablespoons butter
2 teaspoons vanilla extract
3 large eggs
1¼ cups granulated sugar

4 large, ripe peaches (see Baker's Notebook, page 31)
2 tablespoons granulated sugar
½ teaspoon vanilla extract
Wild Berry Whipped Cream (page 251)

1. Make the Hot-Milk Spongecake: Preheat the oven to 350°F., arranging a rack in the middle position. Lightly coat two 9-inch cake pans with nonstick vegetable-oil spray. Line the bottoms with circles of baking parchment.

2. Sift the flour, baking powder and salt together 3 times.

3. In a small saucepan, cook the milk and butter over medium heat, stirring occasionally, until the mixture just barely starts to boil and the butter is melted. Remove from the heat and add the vanilla.

4. Using an electric mixer, beat the eggs and sugar until pale yellow, fluffy and doubled in volume. Continue beating, and drizzle in the hot milk mixture. Fold in the flour mixture.

5. Divide the batter between the two pans and spread evenly. Bake at 350°F. for 20 minutes, or until golden. The centers should spring back when lightly pressed and a cake tester inserted in the centers should come out clean. Transfer the pans to a rack to cool.

6. Run the tip of a knife around the edges of the cakes to loosen them and turn them out of the pans. Trim the tops flat and level with a long serrated knife.

7. Slice the peaches around their creases and twist them into halves. With a spoon, pry out the pits. Slice into ½-inch wedges. In a large bowl, toss with the sugar and vanilla.

8. Lay half of the sliced peaches over one layer of cake, then spread a ½-inch layer of whipped cream on top. Cover with the second layer of cake. Repeat with the remaining peaches and whipped cream.

VARIATION

STRAWBERRY WHIPPED CREAM CAKE For a true, diner-style strawberry shortcake, just substitute strawberries (or any combination of berries) for the peaches.

> The "beaten biscuit" probably originated in Maryland but was made famous in Alabama. It used no leavening agents at all. Air was just "beaten" into it, very often with the handle or side of an ax. And how many whacks were needed to accomplish this task? "Two hundred for home folks . . . five hundred for guests."

hazelnut CHIFFON

Chiffon cakes taste rich and elegant but are actually light, easy and low in fat. The chiffon cake was invented in 1927 by Harry Baker, a Los Angeles insurance salesman, who was soon swamped with cake orders from all of the Hollywood hot spots. In 1947, Betty Crocker bought the formula and claimed in their advertising blitz that it was "the biggest cake-making news in a century." So, next time an insurance agent calls you, don't hang up. He might have a great recipe for you. My version of this sublime creation has been pumped up a notch with a tiny bit of butter and cream.

MAKES ONE 9-INCH CAKE

Nonstick vegetable-oil spray

$^1/_2$ cup cake flour

1 teaspoon baking powder

$^1/_4$ teaspoon salt, plus a pinch for the egg whites

1 cup granulated sugar

$^1/_2$ cup finely chopped, roasted hazelnuts (see page 10)

$^1/_2$ cup vegetable oil

4 large eggs, separated

$^1/_4$ cup heavy cream

2 tablespoons hazelnut liqueur, such as Frangelico

2 tablespoons butter, melted

Pinch of cream of tartar

$^1/_4$ cup raspberry or apricot preserves

Confectioners' sugar, for dusting

1. Preheat the oven to 350°F., arranging a rack in the middle position. Lightly coat two 9-inch round cake pans with nonstick vegetable-oil spray. Line the bottoms with circles of baking parchment.

2. In a large mixing bowl, sift the flour, baking powder, $^1/_4$ teaspoon salt, and $^1/_2$ cup of the sugar together 3 times. Stir in the chopped hazelnuts. Form a well in the center and add the oil, egg yolks, cream, hazelnut liqueur and butter. Mix together until just blended.

3. In a clean, dry mixing bowl, whisk the egg whites with the pinches of salt and cream of tartar until creamy, foamy and barely able to hold peaks (yes, you may use an electric mixer). While sprinkling in the remaining ½ cup of sugar, continue whisking until the whites are the consistency of shaving cream.

4. Fold a third of the egg whites into the hazelnut and yolk mixture, then fold in the remainder of the whites.

5. Divide the batter between the two pans and spread evenly. Bake at 350°F. for 20 minutes, or until golden. The centers should spring back when lightly pressed and a cake tester inserted in the centers should come out clean. Transfer the pans to a rack to cool.

6. Turn the cake out of the pans and trim the tops flat and even with a large serrated knife. Spread the preserves on one layer, then top with the second layer. Dust with confectioners' sugar.

VARIATION

ALMOND CHIFFON CAKE Substitute toasted, finely chopped almonds (see page 10) for the hazelnuts, and use almond liqueur, such as Amaretto di Saronno, for the hazelnut liqueur.

lemon chiffon CAKE

Here's another terrific cake, ideal for just about any occasion. The light lemon cake is perfectly complemented by the fruity raspberry preserves.

MAKES ONE 9-INCH CAKE

Nonstick vegetable-oil spray
1 cup cake flour
$1/2$ teaspoon baking powder
$1/2$ teaspoon baking soda
$1/4$ teaspoon salt, plus a pinch for the egg whites
1 cup granulated sugar
$1/2$ cup vegetable oil
4 large eggs, separated
$1/4$ cup heavy cream
Grated zest of 3 lemons (about 3 tablespoons zest)
$1/4$ cup fresh lemon juice (from 2 lemons)
2 tablespoons butter, melted
Pinch of cream of tartar
$1/4$ cup raspberry preserves
Confectioners' sugar, for dusting

1. Preheat the oven to 350°F., arranging a rack in the middle position. Lightly coat two 9-inch round cake pans with nonstick vegetable-oil spray. Line the bottoms with circles of baking parchment.

2. In a large mixing bowl, sift the flour, baking powder, baking soda, $1/4$ teaspoon salt, and $1/2$ cup of the sugar together 3 times. Form a well in the center and add the oil, egg yolks, cream, lemon zest, lemon juice and butter. Mix together until just blended.

3. In a clean, dry mixing bowl, whisk the egg whites with the pinches of salt and cream of tartar until creamy, foamy and barely able to hold peaks (yes, you may use an electric mixer). While sprinkling in the remaining $1/2$ cup of sugar, whisk until the consistency of shaving cream.

4. Fold a third of the egg whites into the lemon and yolk mixture, then fold in the remainder of the whites just until blended.

5. Divide the batter between the two pans and spread evenly. Bake at 350°F. for 20 minutes, or until golden. The centers should spring back when lightly pressed and a cake tester inserted in the centers should come out clean. Transfer the pans to a rack to cool.

6. Turn the cakes out of the pans and trim the tops flat and even with a large serrated knife. Spread the raspberry preserves on one layer, then top with the second layer. Dust with confectioners' sugar.

VARIATION

COFFEE CHIFFON CAKE Substitute ¼ cup coffee liqueur plus 2 tablespoons instant espresso dissolved in a tablespoon of hot water for the lemon zest and lemon juice. Use raspberry or, alternatively, apricot preserves.

gingerbread CAKE

George Washington chopped down a cherry tree, brought the mighty British army to its knees and oversaw the creation of what would become the most powerful nation on earth. But his mom . . . boy, could she bake gingerbread! Even before she was known as the mother of the father of our nation, she was renowned for baking up a deliciously spicy gingerbread. Although this is not Mama Washington's own personal recipe, it is the kind of moist and sticky cake-style gingerbread that she would have been proud to have made. This cake is great on its own but even better with cream cheese and date frosting.

MAKES ONE 13 × 9-INCH CAKE

GINGERBREAD CAKE
Nonstick vegetable-oil spray
1 3-inch piece of ginger, peeled
2½ cups cake flour
1½ teaspoons baking soda
1 teaspoon ground ginger
1 teaspoon ground cinnamon
1 teaspoon ground cloves
½ teaspoon salt
½ cup plus 2 tablespoons apple cider
½ cup blackstrap molasses (see Baker's Notebook, below)
½ teaspoon vanilla extract
1 cup (2 sticks) unsalted butter, at room temperature
¾ cup granulated sugar
1 large egg

CREAM CHEESE AND DATE FROSTING
8 ounces cream cheese, at room temperature
1 teaspoon ground cinnamon
½ cup confectioners' sugar
½ teaspoon vanilla extract
¾ cup coarsely chopped dates

1. Preheat the oven to 350°F., arranging a rack in the middle position. Lightly coat a 13 × 9-inch cake pan with nonstick vegetable-oil spray. Line the bottom with baking parchment.

2. Finely grate the fresh ginger with a box grater or a Microplane grater. Set aside.

3. Sift the flour, baking soda, ground ginger, cinnamon, cloves and salt together 3 times and set aside.

4. In a small saucepan, cook the cider until it just starts to boil. Remove from the heat and stir in the molasses and vanilla.

5. Using an electric mixer, beat the butter and sugar together at high speed for 15 seconds, or until combined. Add the egg and continue beating until light and fluffy, about 6 minutes.

6. With the mixer on its lowest setting, beat in a third of the flour mixture. Beat in half of the cider mixture and the grated ginger and its juice. Beat in another third of the flour mixture. Beat in the remaining cider and then the remaining flour mixture.

7. Spread the batter in the pan and bake at 350°F. for 30 minutes, or until the center springs back when lightly pressed and a cake tester inserted in the center comes out clean. Transfer the pan to a rack to cool.

8. Make the Cream Cheese and Date Frosting: Using an electric mixer, beat the cream cheese, cinnamon, confectioners' sugar and vanilla at low speed until blended, then increase the speed and beat until fluffy. Mix in the dates.

9. Turn the cake out of the pan. Invert onto a platter and frost, or just spread the frosting on and serve straight out of the pan.

NOTEBOOK

BAKER'S

The very best way to peel ginger is to scrape the skin off with a teaspoon.

Blackstrap molasses is a thick, intensely flavored molasses. It is available in health food stores and some supermarkets. Sometimes it's labeled as "robust."

ORANGE & ALMOND cake

When the first Spanish explorers toured Florida, they brought orange and lemon seeds with them. Searching for gold and elixirs of youth, however, had higher priority on their travel itinerary than the planting of citrus groves. They ended up discarding the seeds and, years later . . . surprise! Orange and lemon trees were growing wild, all over the place. Eventually, they made it all the way to California. This buttery comfort cake has a refreshing citrus zip, reminiscent of a Creamsicle. It also has great crunch since it gets smothered in toasted California almonds.

MAKES ONE 9-INCH CAKE

Nonstick vegetable-oil spray

1½ cups cake flour

¾ teaspoon baking powder

½ teaspoon baking soda

¼ teaspoon salt

½ cup (1 stick) unsalted butter, at room temperature

1 cup granulated sugar

Grated zest of 1 orange (about 2 tablespoons zest)

2 large eggs

½ cup buttermilk

1 teaspoon vanilla extract

1 teaspoon almond extract

2 tablespoons orange liqueur or 1 teaspoon orange extract

¼ cup thawed orange juice concentrate

ORANGE BUTTERCREAM

½ cup (1 stick) unsalted butter, at room temperature

½ cup vegetable shortening

Grated zest of 2 oranges (about ¼ cup zest)

1 pound confectioners' sugar, sifted (about 5 cups)

2 tablespoons orange liqueur or 1 teaspoon orange extract

½ cup sliced almonds, lightly toasted (see page 10)

1. Preheat the oven to 350°F., arranging a rack in the middle position. Lightly coat two 9-inch round cake pans with nonstick vegetable-oil spray. Line the bottoms with circles of baking parchment.

2. Sift the flour, baking powder, baking soda and salt together 3 times and set aside.

3. Using an electric mixer, beat the butter, sugar and orange zest together at high speed for 15 seconds, or until combined. Add the eggs, one at a time, beating until each is incorporated. Continue beating until light and fluffy, about 5 more minutes.

4. With the mixer on its lowest setting, beat in a third of the flour mixture. Beat in the buttermilk, vanilla, almond extract and orange liqueur, then another third of the flour mixture. Beat in the orange juice concentrate and then the remaining flour.

5. Divide the batter between the two pans and spread evenly. Bake at 350°F. for 20 minutes, or until golden brown. The centers should spring back when lightly pressed and a cake tester inserted in the centers should come out clean. Transfer the pans to a rack to cool.

6. Make the Orange Buttercream: Using an electric mixer, beat together the butter, vegetable shortening and orange zest until blended. With the mixer running, gradually add the confectioners' sugar until incorporated. Add the orange liqueur and beat until light and fluffy, about 5 more minutes.

7. Turn the cakes out of the pans and trim the tops flat and even with a large serrated knife. Spread 1/2 inch of frosting on one layer, then stack the other on top. Frost the top and sides of the cake with the remaining frosting. Coat the sides with the toasted almonds.

VARIATIONS

Try substituting chopped and lightly toasted hazelnuts, pistachios or shredded coconut for the almonds. For a lovely decoration, top the cake with white chocolate curls. For a real orange kick, spread 1/4 cup of orange marmalade between the layers.

apple & pear SKILLET CAKE

In the old days, many families didn' t have special pans just for cakes, so they baked cakes like this one in an iron skillet. With juicy, caramelized fruit on top and moist and spicy cake on the bottom, this skillet cake lies deliciously between a French tarte Tatin and an upside-down cake.

MAKES ONE 10-INCH CAKE

CARAMEL APPLE & PEAR TOPPING

6 tablespoons unsalted butter

3/4 cup granulated sugar

2 tart baking apples, such as Granny Smith, Rome, Golden Delicious or Northern
    Spy, peeled, cored and sliced into 8 wedges per fruit

2 Bartlett or Anjou pears, peeled, cored and sliced into 8 wedges per fruit

YELLOW CAKE

1 1/2 cups cake flour

1 1/2 teaspoons baking powder

1/2 teaspoon ground cinnamon

1/4 teaspoon ground nutmeg

1/4 teaspoon salt

6 tablespoons unsalted butter, at room temperature

1 cup granulated sugar

2 large eggs

1/2 cup milk

1/4 cup cream sherry

1 teaspoon vanilla extract

Nonstick vegetable-oil spray

1. Preheat the oven to 375°F., arranging a rack in the middle position.

2. Make the Caramel Apple & Pear Topping: In a 10-inch, ovenproof skillet over medium-high heat, melt the butter and sugar together until just bubbling. Remove from the heat and alternate the apple and pear wedges in a tight pinwheel around the outer edge of the pan. Fill the center with the remaining slices (especially any broken or odd-shaped pieces).

3. Make the Yellow Cake: Sift the flour, baking powder, cinnamon, nutmeg and salt together 3 times and set aside.

4. Using an electric mixer, beat the butter and sugar together at high speed for 15 seconds, or until combined. Add the eggs one at a time, beating until each is incorporated. Continue beating until light and fluffy, about 5 minutes more.

5. With the mixer on its lowest setting, beat in a third of the flour mixture. Beat in half of the milk, the sherry and vanilla, then another third of the flour mixture. Beat in the remaining milk and then the remaining flour mixture.

6. Lightly coat the exposed inner surface of the skillet with vegetable-oil spray. Spread the batter evenly over the fruit. Bake at 375°F. for 45 minutes, or until golden brown and the center springs back when lightly pressed. Transfer the pan to a rack, and let cool for 2 minutes.

7. Run a knife around the edge of the pan and invert a serving plate over it. Carefully (no, make that *very carefully*) flip the plate-covered pan over. If any fruit is stuck to the pan, scrape it off with a spoon and rearrange it on top of the cake. Let cool for 10 minutes before serving.

BAKER'S NOTEBOOK

Pans with plastic or wooden handles won't work for a skillet cake, since they have to go into the oven. Also, a 10-inch slope-sided sauté pan may not be big enough to hold all of the batter. If you use one, just fill it with batter only three quarters of the way up. Cast iron is a great heat conductor and a good choice, but be careful when you invert and unmold the cake. It may be a bit heavy. If you don't have an ovenproof skillet, you can also make the butter-sugar syrup in a saucepan and then pour it into the bottom of a warm 10-inch cake pan. Proceed with the rest of the recipe, setting up the fruit and batter in the cake pan and increasing the baking time to 55 minutes.

You may make this cake with apples or pears alone as well. If you are in a particularly adventurous mood, try substituting Asian pears in this recipe. Their crisp consistency and exotic citrus and berry flavor work wonderfully in this cake.

HAPPY BIRTHDAY cake

Buttermilk cake is the final ingredient for a perfect birthday party. It is moist and flavorful with a crumbly texture that makes it the quintessential American cake. Combine it with this easy, ersatz buttercream and all you will need are the candles. French, Italian and Swiss buttercreams all incorporate butter, sugar and eggs, each in its own respective and fairly complicated method. There is, however, another very simple and extremely flavorful buttercream that is sometimes referred to as "American." It is the embodiment of American baking: simple, to the point and utterly scrumptious.

This is a large batch of batter that should be baked in 9-inch pans. For an 8-inch cake, use the Buttermilk Cake recipe on page 134.

MAKES ONE 9-INCH CAKE

BUTTERMILK CAKE

Nonstick vegetable-oil spray

2^1/$_2$ cups cake flour

1^1/$_2$ teaspoons baking powder

^{1}/$_2$ teaspoon baking soda

^{1}/$_4$ teaspoon salt

^{3}/$_4$ cup (1^1/$_2$ sticks) unsalted butter, at room temperature

1^1/$_2$ cups granulated sugar

3 large eggs

1^1/$_2$ teaspoons vanilla extract

1 cup buttermilk

^{1}/$_2$ teaspoon lemon or orange oil or extract

AMERICAN BUTTERCREAM

^{1}/$_2$ cup vegetable shortening

^{1}/$_2$ cup unsalted butter, at room temperature

1 pound confectioners' sugar, about 4 cups

1 teaspoon vanilla extract

1. Make the Buttermilk Cake: Preheat the oven to 350°F., arranging a rack in the middle position. Lightly coat two 9-inch round cake pans with nonstick vegetable-oil spray and line the bottoms with circles of baking parchment.

2. Sift the flour, baking powder, baking soda and salt together 3 times. Set aside.

3. Using an electric mixer, beat the butter and sugar together at high speed for 15 seconds, or until combined. Add the eggs, one at a time, beating until each is incorporated. Continue beating until light and fluffy, about 5 minutes more.

4. With the mixer on its lowest setting, beat in one third of the flour mixture. Beat in the vanilla and half of the buttermilk, then another third of the flour. Beat in the rest of the buttermilk and then the remaining flour mixture.

5. Divide the batter between the two pans and spread evenly. Bake at 350°F. for 35 minutes, or until the center springs back when lightly pressed and a cake tester comes out clean. Transfer the pans to a rack to cool.

6. Make the American Buttercream: Using an electric mixer, beat together the butter and vegetable shortening until blended. With the mixer running, gradually add the confectioners' sugar until incorporated. Add the vanilla extract and beat until light and fluffy, about 5 more minutes.

7. Turn the cakes out of the pans and trim the tops flat and even with a large serrated knife. Spread ½ inch of frosting on one layer, then stack the other on top. Use the remaining frosting to frost the top and sides of the cake and to pipe a decorative border around the top rim of the cake.

Indian Pudding ★ Berry Bread Pudding ★ Pecan Bread Pudding ★

Butter Pecan–Banana Pudding ★ Rice Pudding ★ Chocolate Malted

Pudding ★ Orange Tapioca Pudding ★ Maple-Oatmeal Cup Custard

★ Vanilla–Brown Sugar Cup Custard ★ Chocolate Cup Custard ★

Dried Plum Whip

puddings
&
custards

The first course served at the first Thanksgiving was a corn-meal and whortleberry pudding, thus establishing a common ground, where Indian corn mush met the British pudding pot. Even though they sharply disagreed on when it should be eaten, the fathers of our nation were all big fans of pudding. The Federalists kept to the old English custom of having it as a first course. The Democrats symbolically broke with tradition and enjoyed their puddings at the end of the meal.

To the British, the word pudding itself can mean dessert, but American puddings—homespun, flavorful and considerably lighter—have come quite a long way from their steamy, fat-laden English ancestors. Many of our most popular puddings, such as chocolate and rice puddings, are more like French pastry creams: smooth, cool and refreshing.

This chapter also includes several recipes for custards, many of which originated in Spain and voyaged to our shores via England. Of course the flans and natillas of the American Southwest are direct descendants of Spain's flans and crema Catalana.

TIPS

In the mid-twentieth century, premixed puddings nearly supplanted the home-made kinds. Yes, boxed pudding mixes are easy to use, but the end result is not nearly as sublime as the real thing. Following a few simple tips will make preparing puddings from scratch a breeze.

★ **To help dissolve cornstarch and other thickeners, whisk them into the liquid, wait 1 minute, then whisk again.**

★ **Be sure to mix any hot liquids into eggs gradually. This process, called tempering, prevents the eggs from becoming prematurely cooked and scrambled. It results in puddings and custards that are smooth and not lumpy or grainy.**

★ **To prevent a skin from forming on your pudding, cover it with waxed paper (not plastic wrap) while it cools. The pudding will seal but still breathe enough so it doesn't become watery.**

★ **Adding a little sugar to milk as you heat it prevents it from scorching on the bottom of the pot.**

★ **Stir, whisk and scrape the bottom of your pot continuously to keep the starch from sticking and burning.**

indian PUDDING

Indian pudding, also known as cornmeal pudding, was one of the earliest Colonial dishes to use indigenous American ingredients. It was popular from Jamestown to Plymouth, but the version we now know is a trademark of the New England Yankee cooking of the nineteenth and twentieth centuries. Places like the Miss Flo Diner, in Florence, Massachusetts, built their reputations on it, and the Boston restaurant Durgin-Park, established in 1826 and still going strong, has served its famous version of this creamy, ethereal pudding for more than 140 years.

Adding cream and sugar helps to prevent the sticky cornmeal from scorching on the bottom of the pot, so the tedious process of heating over a double boiler is unnecessary. This greatly reduces the time needed to make this pudding. Make sure you cook over low heat and scrape the bottom of the pot frequently to keep it from scorching. Substituting dried cranberries (sometimes called craisins) for the typical raisins gives this version a real lift.

This pudding is wonderful served with Lemon Buttermilk Custard Sauce (page 245), Brown Sugar Custard Sauce (page 246), Whipped Cream (page 250), Vanilla Malt Ice Cream (page 230) or store-bought vanilla ice cream.

SERVES 8

2 cups milk

2 cups heavy or whipping cream

¼ cup granulated sugar

1 cup sweet Madeira

2 tablespoons unsalted butter

½ cup fine yellow or white cornmeal

½ cup lightly packed dark brown sugar

½ teaspoon ground cinnamon

½ teaspoon ground ginger

½ teaspoon ground nutmeg

1 large egg

3 large egg yolks

1 teaspoon vanilla extract

½ cup dried cranberries

"It is a barbarous New England custom to serve [Indian Pudding] with vanilla ice cream."

—Joy of Cooking

1. Preheat the oven to 300°F., arranging a rack in the lower third of the oven.

2. In a medium, heavy-bottomed saucepan, bring the milk, 1 cup of the cream, sugar, Madeira, butter and cornmeal to a simmer over medium heat, stirring occasionally so the cornmeal does not stick to the bottom of the pot. Turn the heat down as low as possible and, stirring occasionally, cook for 12 more minutes.

3. While the cornmeal cooks, put the brown sugar, cinnamon, ginger, nutmeg, egg, and yolks in a medium bowl and whisk just to blend. Gradually whisk in the hot corn mush to warm the egg mixture slowly. Mix in the vanilla and dried cranberries. Divide the pudding among eight 5-ounce ramekins.

4. Put the ramekins into a roasting pan and drizzle 2 tablespoons of the remaining cream on top of each pudding. Add enough hot water to the roasting pan to come halfway up the sides of the ramekins, and cover the pan tightly with aluminum foil. Bake at 300°F. for 35 to 45 minutes, until the puddings are set.

5. Serve warm, with the topping of your choice.

BAKER'S NOTEBOOK

This pudding can also be made in a 2-quart baking dish. Follow all directions but increase the baking time to 1 to 1¼ hours.

BERRY bread pudding

Serve this warm and satisfying custard bread pudding with Lemon Buttermilk Custard Sauce (page 245), Brown Sugar Custard Sauce (page 246), or Whiskey & Molasses Sauce (page 247).

SERVES 8

2 cups milk

1 cup heavy cream

1½ cups granulated sugar

4 large eggs

4 large egg yolks

2 tablespoons raspberry liqueur, such as Framboise, or elderberry cordial

1 loaf of stale bread (1 pound), cut into ¾-inch cubes

1 pint fresh or 2 cups frozen raspberries, blackberries or blueberries

1. Preheat the oven to 300°F., arranging a rack in the middle position.

2. In a medium, heavy-bottomed saucepan, cook the milk, cream and ¼ cup of sugar over medium heat, stirring occasionally, until it just barely starts to boil, about 4 minutes.

3. Put the remaining 1¼ cups of sugar, the eggs, egg yolks and liqueur in a large bowl and gently whisk just to blend. Gradually whisk in the hot cream mixture to warm the egg mixture slowly. Mix in the bread cubes and set aside for 15 minutes, until the cubes soak up all of the eggy liquid. Fold in the berries, then transfer the mixture to a 2-quart baking dish.

4. Set the baking dish into a roasting pan and add enough hot water to the roasting pan to come about 1 inch up the side of the baking dish. Cover the roasting pan tightly with foil and bake at 300°F. for 45 minutes. Remove the foil and bake for 15 more minutes, until lightly tanned, slightly puffed and firm. Serve warm with your choice of sauce.

BAKER'S NOTEBOOK

You may serve your bread pudding right away but it is best the next day. Let it cool down, then refrigerate overnight. To serve, reheat in a 325°F. oven for 15 minutes.

pecan BREAD PUDDING

The ready supply of sugar from local refineries and the "savoir faire" of Creole cuisine added up to New Orleans classics like this nutty, moist bread pudding. Make sure that you serve it with Whiskey & Molasses Sauce (page 247), Brown Sugar Custard Sauce (page 246) or Orange Hard Sauce (page 248).

SERVES 8

2 cups milk

1 cup heavy cream

$3/4$ cup granulated sugar

1 cup lightly packed dark brown sugar

4 large eggs

4 large egg yolks

2 tablespoons dark rum

2 tablespoons molasses

1 loaf of stale bread (1 pound), cut into $3/4$-inch cubes

1 cup lightly toasted pecans (see page 10)

1. Preheat the oven to 300°F., arranging a rack in the middle position.

2. In a medium, heavy-bottomed saucepan, cook the milk, cream and granulated sugar over medium heat, stirring occasionally, until the mixture just barely starts to boil, about 4 minutes.

3. Put the brown sugar, eggs, egg yolks, rum and molasses in a large bowl and gently whisk just to blend. Gradually whisk in the hot cream mixture to warm the egg mixture slowly. Mix in the bread cubes and set aside for 15 minutes, until the cubes soak up all of the eggy liquid. Fold in the pecans, then transfer the mixture to a 2-quart baking dish.

4. Set the baking dish into a roasting pan and add enough hot water to the roasting pan to come about 1 inch up the side of the baking dish. Cover the roasting pan tightly with foil and bake at 300°F. for 45 minutes. Remove the foil and bake for 15 more minutes, until lightly tanned, slightly puffed and firm. Serve warm with your choice of sauce.

butter pecan-BANANA PUDDING

This homestyle pudding is, in reality, a simplified Southern version of traditional English trifle with vanilla wafer cookies standing in for the pound cake. Like so many American descendants of English desserts, it became chock-full of luscious flavor when it crossed the Atlantic. The smooth pudding and bananas mixed with crisp vanilla wafers make a lovely textural contrast. It is usually made with vanilla pudding, but butter pecan makes this version extra special.

SERVES 8

¹⁄₄ cup cornstarch

2 cups milk

1 teaspoon vanilla extract

1 tablespoon dark rum

¹⁄₂ cup granulated sugar

2 tablespoons molasses

4 large egg yolks

2 tablespoons unsalted butter

1 cup lightly toasted and coarsely chopped pecans (see page 10)

4 ounces vanilla wafers

3¹⁄₂ ripe bananas, peeled and sliced ¹⁄₂ inch thick

Whipped Cream (page 250)

1. In a medium bowl, whisk the cornstarch into ¹⁄₂ cup of the milk. Let rest for 1 minute, then whisk in the vanilla, rum, ¹⁄₄ cup of the sugar and the molasses. Whisk in the egg yolks and set aside.

2. In a medium, heavy-bottomed saucepan, cook the remaining 1¹⁄₂ cups milk and the remaining ¹⁄₄ cup sugar over medium heat, stirring occasionally, until the mixture just barely starts to boil, about 4 minutes. While gently whisking the hot milk mixture, slowly drizzle the egg mixture into it until completely incorporated. While constantly whisking and scraping the bottom of the pot, cook until tiny bubbles boil up continuously for 10 seconds. Mix in the butter. Strain, then mix in ³⁄₄ cup of the pecans. Cover with waxed paper and let cool, then refrigerate.

3. In a 6-cup glass bowl or serving dish, alternately layer the vanilla wafers and bananas between ¼-inch-thick layers of pudding, repeating until you reach the top of the bowl, reserving a few wafers for garnish. Cover the pudding with waxed paper and place in the refrigerator for 2 to 6 hours to set.

4. To serve, top with whipped cream, a few crumbled wafers and the remaining ¼ cup of pecans.

> **Besides berries and Concord grapes, there are almost no fruits native to North America. The first dessert was probably the concoction made by Iroquois and Algonquins in upstate New York and Vermont—dried popcorn, drizzled with maple syrup.**

RICE pudding

There are a lot of exotic rice pudding recipes floating around today and many have their merits, but this simple, classic version always seems the best to me.

SERVES 6 TO 8

3/4 cup rice, preferably short-grain, Japanese style (see Baker's Notebook)

1 vanilla bean

2 cups milk

1 cup light cream

3/4 cup granulated sugar

1 large egg

2 large egg yolks

1/4 cup lightly packed light brown sugar

1 tablespoon dark rum

1 teaspoon vanilla extract

1. In a medium saucepan, bring 2½ cups of water to a boil. Add the rice and reduce heat to low. Cover and cook for 25 to 30 minutes, or until the water is just absorbed.

2. Split the vanilla bean lengthwise and scrape out the seeds. Stir the seeds, bean halves, milk, cream and sugar into the rice. Cover, bring to a simmer, and cook for another 15 minutes.

3. Put the egg, yolks, brown sugar, rum and vanilla in a medium bowl and whisk just to blend. Gradually whisk in the hot rice mixture to warm the egg mixture slowly. Return the mixture to the saucepan and, while constantly whisking and scraping the bottom of the pot, cook over medium heat until tiny bubbles boil up continuously for 10 seconds.

4. Transfer to a bowl and let cool. Remove the vanilla bean halves and discard. Refrigerate the pudding, then serve chilled.

NOTEBOOK

BAKER'S Starchy texture and sweet but robust flavor make Japanese-style rice perfect for rice pudding. It is available in Asian markets, where you can find brands that are grown right here in the States. Another good choice is Italian Arborio rice.

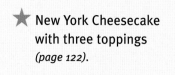 New York Cheesecake
with three toppings
(page 122).

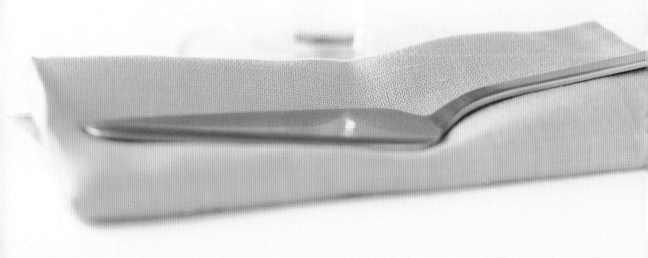

★ Chocolate Icebox Cake
(page 120).

★ Peach Shortcake
(page 136).

Butter Pecan–Banana Pudding
(page 158).

★ Tropical Fruits Foster
(page 238).

right: Bourbon Snaps *(page 204)*.
below: Benne Wafers *(page 198)*.
bottom: Molasses "Cry Baby"
Lace Cookies *(page 201)*.

★ **top:** Chocolate-Coconut Bars *(page 216)*.
middle: Lemon Bars with Pecan Crust *(page 212)*.
bottom: Blondies *(page 209)*.

★ **clockwise, from above:**
Chocolate Glazed Doughnuts *(page 180)*,
Jelly Doughnuts *(page 178)*.
Cake Doughnuts *(page 172)*.

chocolate malted PUDDING

Long ago, chocolate pudding was a "from scratch" treat. But recent generations have been convinced that it can only be made from a box of premixed ingredients. Today, thanks to the food revolution of the 1980s, chocolate pudding has once again regained its home-made status. Try this "old-school" method, and you will become an instant convert.

SERVES 6

4 ounces milk chocolate, coarsely chopped

2 tablespoons unsalted butter

2 tablespoons cornstarch

$\frac{1}{4}$ cup unsweetened Dutch-processed cocoa powder

$\frac{1}{4}$ cup plain malted milk powder (such as Carnation brand)

1 teaspoon vanilla extract

$\frac{1}{2}$ cup granulated sugar

2$\frac{1}{2}$ cups milk

1 large egg

2 large egg yolks

1. Melt the chocolate and butter in a completely dry bowl or double boiler set over barely simmering water, stirring occasionally.

2. In a medium bowl, whisk the cornstarch, cocoa, malt powder, vanilla and $\frac{1}{4}$ cup of the sugar into $\frac{1}{2}$ cup of the milk, then whisk in the egg and yolks.

3. In a medium, heavy-bottomed saucepan, cook the remaining 2 cups milk and the remaining $\frac{1}{4}$ cup sugar over medium heat, stirring occasionally, until the mixture just barely starts to boil, about 4 minutes. While whisking the hot milk mixture, slowly drizzle the egg mixture into it until completely incorporated. While constantly whisking and scraping the bottom of the pan, cook until tiny bubbles boil up continuously for 5 seconds. Remove from heat and strain.

4. Thoroughly mix in the melted chocolate. Divide the pudding among 6 serving bowls (or pour into one big one). Place a piece of waxed paper directly on the surface of each of the puddings to prevent a skin from forming. Let cool for 1 hour, then refrigerate until chilled.

ORANGE tapioca pudding

Tapioca pudding is one of those old-fashioned desserts that, until recently, had all but disappeared from our tables. Lucky for all of us, it has recently been revived by several of the best pastry chefs in America. Tapioca is made from the starchy part of the tropical cassava root. This recipe uses quick or granulated tapioca. It won' t work with the instant or pearl varieties.

SERVES 6 TO 8

½ cup quick or granulated tapioca
3 cups milk
Grated zest of 1 orange (about 2 tablespoons)
¾ cup sugar
1 large egg
2 large egg yolks
2 tablespoons orange liqueur or 1 teaspoon orange oil (see Baker's Notebook)
    or extract
½ teaspoon vanilla extract

1. In a medium saucepan, bring the tapioca, milk, orange zest and ¼ cup of the sugar to a boil. Reduce the heat to low and simmer for 2 minutes.

2. Put the egg, yolks, orange flavoring, the remaining ½ cup sugar and the vanilla in a medium bowl and whisk just to blend. Gradually whisk in the hot tapioca mixture to warm the egg mixture slowly. Return the mixture to the saucepan and, while constantly whisking and scraping the bottom of the pot, cook over low heat for 3 minutes, or until tiny bubbles boil up continuously for 10 seconds.

3. Transfer to a bowl and let cool. Refrigerate, then serve chilled.

BAKER'S NOTEBOOK

Orange oil, made by Boyajian, is available in specialty stores. It has a very pure orange-zest flavor.

MAPLE-OATMEAL cup custard

What could be more luxurious and seductive than a rich custard? What could be more home-spun, unpretentious and comforting than oatmeal with maple syrup? In this delicious cup custard, the two combine. For the best texture, use quick-cooking (not instant) oatmeal.

For an extra added attraction, place some thinly sliced bananas on top of each custard. Sprinkle with a teaspoon of sugar and caramelize by placing under a hot broiler for 15 seconds or passing the tip of a propane torch over the top.

SERVES 8

¾ cup milk
2 cups light or heavy cream
1 teaspoon granulated sugar
¼ cup quick-cooking rolled oats
6 large egg yolks
½ cup pure maple syrup
Fresh berries, to garnish

1. Preheat the oven to 300°F., arranging a rack in the middle position.

2. In a medium, heavy-bottomed saucepan, bring the milk, cream, sugar, and oatmeal to a simmer over medium heat. Cook for 3 minutes, stirring occasionally so the mixture does not stick to the bottom of the pot.

3. Put the egg yolks and maple syrup in a medium bowl and whisk just to blend. Gently whisk in the oatmeal mixture, a glob at a time. Divide the pudding among eight 6-ounce ramekins.

4. Put the ramekins in a roasting pan and add enough hot water to the pan to come halfway up the sides of the ramekins. Cover the pan tightly with aluminum foil. Bake at 300°F. for 35 to 45 minutes, until the custards are barely set and jiggly. Place the whole pan on a rack and let cool to room temperature.

5. Remove the ramekins from the water bath and refrigerate for 2 hours or overnight. Serve with fresh berries.

vanilla-brown sugar
CUP CUSTARD

Custards have a contradictory appeal. They are luscious, sophisticated and sensual, but also simple, old-fashioned and kid friendly. This custard is as rich as a crème brûlée yet downright homey and completely unaffected. Don't stand on ceremony—just grab a spoon and dig in!

SERVES 6

1 vanilla bean

2 cups heavy cream

¼ cup granulated sugar

6 large egg yolks

½ cup lightly packed light brown sugar

1 teaspoon vanilla extract

1 tablespoon dark rum

1. Preheat the oven to 300°F., arranging a rack in the middle position.

2. Split the vanilla bean lengthwise and scrape out the seeds. In a medium, heavy-bottomed saucepan, cook the seeds, bean halves, cream and sugar over medium heat, stirring occasionally, until the mixture just barely starts to boil, about 4 minutes.

3. Put the egg yolks, brown sugar, vanilla extract and rum in a medium bowl and whisk just to blend. Gradually whisk in the hot cream mixture to warm the egg mixture slowly. Strain the custard and divide it evenly among six 6-ounce ramekins.

4. Put the ramekins in a roasting pan and add enough hot water to the pan to come halfway up the sides of the ramekins. Cover the pan tightly with aluminum foil. Bake at 300°F. for 35 to 45 minutes, until the custards are barely set and jiggly. Place the whole pan on a rack and let cool to room temperature.

5. Remove the ramekins from the water bath and refrigerate for 2 hours or overnight.

BUTTER PECAN CUP CUSTARD Whisk 1 tablespoon of molasses into the egg mixture. Mix 1 tablespoon of coarsely chopped, toasted pecans (see page 10) into each custard cup before baking. After the custard is set, sprinkle another tablespoon of toasted pecans on top.

The ultimate custard dessert is, of course, crème brûlée. Although Spain (not France) is the most probable birthplace of the recipe, some claim that its origin is actually American. Its worldwide popularity is certainly attributable to pastry chef Dieter Schorner and restaurateur Sirio Maccioni, who introduced it in its modern form at the 1974 opening of Le Cirque in New York City.

chocolate CUP CUSTARD

Here's a creamy and comforting custard with an intense wallop of chocolate!

SERVES 6

6 ounces bittersweet chocolate, coarsely chopped
2 cups light, heavy or whipping cream
¼ cup granulated sugar
4 large egg yolks

1. Preheat the oven to 300°F., arranging a rack in the middle position.

2. Melt the chocolate in a completely dry bowl or double boiler set over barely simmering water.

3. In a medium, heavy-bottomed saucepan, cook the cream and 2 tablespoons of the sugar over medium heat, stirring occasionally, until the mixture just barely starts to boil, about 4 minutes.

4. Put the egg yolks and the 2 remaining tablespoons of sugar in a medium bowl and whisk just to blend. Gradually whisk in the hot cream mixture to warm the egg mixture slowly. Strain the custard, then slowly whisk it into the chocolate. Divide it among six 6-ounce ramekins.

5. Put the ramekins in a roasting pan and add enough hot water to the pan to come halfway up the sides of the ramekins. Cover the pan tightly with aluminum foil. Bake at 300°F. for 35 to 45 minutes, until the custards are barely set and jiggly. Place the whole pan on a rack and cool to room temperature.

6. Remove the ramekins from the water bath and refrigerate for 2 hours or overnight.

VARIATION

MILK CHOCOLATE CUP CUSTARD Substitute 6 ounces of coarsely chopped milk chocolate for the bittersweet. Whisk ¼ cup of plain malted milk powder and 1 teaspoon vanilla extract into the egg mixture.

DRIED PLUM whip

Immensely popular in the nineteenth and early twentieth centuries, prune whip—uh, excuse me, dried plum whip—is a lighter version of an English fruit fool. It's a delicious fruit purée folded into fluffy egg whites: light, yummy and (get this) good for you. What a wonderful combo!

SERVES 6 TO 8

18 large pitted prunes (about 1 cup or 5$\frac{1}{2}$ ounces)
$\frac{3}{4}$ cup Japanese plum wine (see Baker's Notebook) or prune juice
4 large egg whites
2 tablespoons granulated sugar
Pinch of salt
Pinch of cream of tartar
$\frac{1}{4}$ cup chopped, roasted hazelnuts (see page 10), optional

1. In a small saucepan over low heat, simmer the prunes in the plum wine and $\frac{1}{2}$ cup of water for 10 minutes, or until very soft. Let cool, then purée in a food processor until smooth. Set aside.

2. Put the egg whites, sugar, salt and cream of tartar in a clean, dry bowl set over a pan of simmering water. Whisk by hand constantly until the temperature of the egg whites is hotter than very hot bath water and they are just starting to steam, 160°F. Remove from heat and continue to whisk (you can now switch to an electric mixer) until the consistency of shaving cream.

3. Fold a third of the egg whites into the prune purée, then gently fold the prunes into the remaining egg whites to create a marbled effect. Refrigerate for 1 hour.

4. Serve in individual glasses, topped with the hazelnuts.

BAKER'S NOTEBOOK
Japanese plum wine is available in most liquor stores. My favorite brand is Fuki.

Cake Doughnuts ★ Chocolate Doughnuts ★ Yeast Doughnuts ★ Jelly Doughnuts ★ Chocolate Glazed Doughnuts ★ Funnel Cakes ★ Apple Fritters

doughnuts

& OTHER FRIED DOUGHS

Car 54, where are you? At the doughnut shop, of course. But stereotypes aside, the fact remains that Americans are wild for doughnuts. So wild, in fact, that we consume 3.7 billion of them a year. Archaeologists have unearthed petrified chunks of fried dough that predate the pueblos of New Mexico. (I think that some of the specimens they sell at the doughnut shop on my corner could qualify as genuine fossils.) Doughnuts as we know them were introduced by Dutch colonists who settled the area around New York's Hudson River, where they called their fried dough *oliekocken,* or oil cakes.

Doughnuts come in all shapes and sizes but basically, they can be divided into two categories. Cake doughnuts are leavened with chemicals like baking powder or soda. Yeast doughnuts get their rising power from air bubbles caused by the fermentation, or "breathing," of yeast.

Unfortunately, doughnuts lose their allure after 3 or 4 hours. When it comes to doughnuts, it's the fresher the better. So, if you want the best, make 'em yourself and serve them right away.

TIPS

Doughnuts are a lot easier to make than you think and actually a whole lot of fun. You can make the dough in advance, cut it out and refrigerate for the next day. Then just wake up, heat the oil and enjoy the best doughnuts that you and your family have ever had.

Here are some hints to consider:

★ You can find one-piece doughnut cutters that cut out the dough and the center hole in one fell swoop. You can also use a larger cookie cutter for the outer circumference of the dough and a 3/4-inch cutter for the center hole.

★ Sticky dough can cling to doughnut or cookie cutters. To avoid a real mess, dip the cutter in flour before stamping out each doughnut.

★ While the dough is resting, heat the oil. At 365°F., the doughnuts will sear, creating a nice outer crust that keeps the oil from soaking in. This will also retain moisture in the doughnuts' interiors. It's a win-win situation.

★ A thermometer will help you to gauge the exact temperature of the oil. If you don't have one, test a small piece of dough. It should bubble up and brown in 1 minute. After you have reached the desired heat, turn the heat down a little to maintain the temperature.

★ Doughnut dough keeps in the refrigerator for up to 2 or 3 days and freezes (well wrapped) for 6 weeks.

cake DOUGHNUTS

In 1920, Adolph Levitt invented an automated doughnut machine. He set it up in the front window of his bake shop, where it cranked out doughnuts for his customers' consumption and entertainment. Today, mechanized doughnut production is the norm. But here is the good news: Classic cake doughnuts (and most others, for that matter) are easy and fun to make at home. You don't need industrial equipment or access to one of Adolph's dough-nut machines. An electric mixer or wooden spoon and bowl will do for beating the batter together. As for the frying, a saucepan of oil and a thermometer will suffice. Try this simple, but scrumptious, recipe. Your coffee break will never be the same.

MAKES 24 DOUGHNUTS

4 cups all-purpose flour
1 tablespoon baking powder
1/2 teaspoon salt
1/2 teaspoon ground cinnamon
1/2 teaspoon ground nutmeg
2 tablespoons unsalted butter, at room temperature
1 cup granulated sugar
3 large eggs
3/4 cup milk
1 tablespoon dark rum, preferably Jamaican
Vegetable oil, preferably canola, for frying
Confectioners' sugar, for dusting

1. Sift together the flour, baking powder, salt, cinnamon and nutmeg. Set aside.

2. In a large bowl, beat together the butter and sugar until blended. Add the eggs, one at a time, beating until each is incorporated.

3. Beat half of the flour mixture into the butter mixture, then add the milk and rum. Finally, beat in the remainder of the flour mixture, forming a soft dough. Cover with plastic wrap and refrigerate for 1 hour.

4. On a lightly floured surface, roll half the dough out in a layer $1/2$ inch thick. If it is too sticky to roll, sprinkle flour on the dough and the rolling pin. With a floured $2^1/_4$-inch doughnut cutter or round cookie cutter (if using the latter, you will also need to cut a center hole with a $3/_4$-inch round cutter), cut out the doughnuts and transfer them to a lightly floured plate or cookie sheet. Lightly cover the doughnuts with plastic wrap and refrigerate for 15 more minutes.

5. Meanwhile, in a deep fryer, heavy saucepan or deep skillet, heat at least $1^1/_2$ inches of oil to 365°F. With a spatula, carefully slide 3 doughnuts into the oil. When their undersides are golden brown, turn them with a slotted spoon or spatula. When the second sides brown, lift them out with a slotted spoon and drain them on paper towels.

6. Dust liberally with confectioners' sugar.

CINNAMON SUGAR

You can also coat your doughnuts with cinnamon sugar.

1 teaspoon cinnamon
$1/_4$ cup granulated sugar

In a paper bag, mix the sugar and cinnamon together. Add the doughnuts, 3 or 4 at a time, and shake, shake, shake.

BAKER'S NOTEBOOK

Canola oil is my first choice for frying. It has an extremely high smoke point, so doughnuts will not pick up any "dirty" oil flavor. Peanut and corn oils are also good choices. Don't use olive oil. It is great on salads but absolutely unsuitable for deep-frying.

chocolate DOUGHNUTS

Rich chocolate flavor and a moist interior—that's what makes a chocolate doughnut a winner. Here's an easy-to-make chocolate doughnut that will become your trademark.

MAKES 30 DOUGHNUTS

4 cups cake flour

$1/2$ cup unsweetened cocoa powder

2 teaspoons baking powder

$1/2$ teaspoon salt

3 tablespoons unsalted butter, at room temperature

$1^1/_2$ cups granulated sugar

2 large eggs

1 teaspoon vanilla extract

$3/_4$ cup milk

Vegetable oil, preferably canola, for frying

Confectioners' sugar, for dusting

1. Sift together the flour, cocoa, baking powder and salt. Set aside.

2. In a large bowl, beat together the butter and sugar until blended. Add the eggs, one at a time, beating until each is incorporated.

3. Beat in half of the flour mixture, then the vanilla and milk. Finally, beat in the remainder of the flour mixture, forming a soft dough. Lightly dust the dough with flour and transfer to a lightly floured cookie sheet. Pat it out in a layer $1/2$ inch thick. If the dough is too sticky, sprinkle more flour over and under it. Lightly cover with plastic wrap and refrigerate for 30 minutes.

4. With a floured $2^1/_4$-inch doughnut cutter or round cookie cutter (if using the latter, you will also need to cut a center hole with a $3/_4$-inch round cutter), cut out the doughnuts and transfer them to a lightly floured plate or cookie sheet. Lightly cover the doughnuts with plastic wrap and refrigerate for 15 more minutes.

5. Meanwhile, in a deep fryer, heavy saucepan or deep skillet, heat at least 2 inches of oil to 365°F. With a spatula, carefully slide 3 doughnuts into the oil. In about 1 minute, the undersides should look craggy and crunchy. Turn the doughnuts with a slotted spoon or spatula. When the second side looks crunchy, lift them out with a slotted spoon and drain on paper towels.

6. Dust liberally with confectioners' sugar.

WHY DOUGHNUTS HAVE HOLES—A Historical Perspective

Washington Irving, in his **History of New York**, gave the Dutch fried oliekocken, or "oil cakes," a new name: "doughnuts." Years later, the hole was added (or subtracted). This amazing feat of culinary engineering increased the crunchy surface area while eliminating the chance of a raw or soggy interior.

YEAST doughnuts

Like their cakey cousins, these yeast-risen doughnuts are a cinch to make and the kind of treat that you just can't stop eating. It is preferable to use bread flour but don't worry, they will still be wonderful if you can only find all-purpose. In Louisiana, they are still called by their French name, beignets.

MAKES 36 DOUGHNUTS

1¼ cups milk

½ ounce fresh (compressed) yeast or one ¼-ounce packet dry yeast

¼ cup granulated sugar

4 cups bread flour or all-purpose flour

2 large eggs

¼ teaspoon salt

¾ cup (1½ sticks) unsalted butter, at room temperature

Vegetable oil, preferably canola, for frying

¼ cup confectioners' sugar

½ teaspoon ground cinnamon

1. In a small saucepan, heat the milk to approximately 105°F., a little above body temperature.

2. In the bowl of an electric mixer fitted with a dough hook, mix together the heated milk, yeast, sugar and 1 cup of the flour. Let rest (or "proof") until bubbly, 10 to 15 minutes.

3. With the mixer on low, add the eggs, then the rest of the flour and the salt. Add the butter and blend to form a smooth, silky dough that pulls away from the sides of the bowl. If it is too wet, add a little more flour. Knead in the mixer for 3 minutes, then transfer to a lightly greased bowl and cover with plastic wrap. Place the dough in a warm area and let rise until doubled in volume, about 1 hour. (You may also let it slow-rise in the refrigerator for 12 hours if you'd like to finish the doughnuts later.)

4. Divide the dough in half. On a lightly floured surface, roll 1 piece out to a ½-inch-thick rectangle. With a knife or pizza wheel, cut into 2½-inch squares. Set on a lightly floured cookie sheet, dust with flour and cover with plastic wrap. Let rise in a warm place for 30 minutes or refrigerate for up to 6 hours. Repeat with the remaining dough.

5. When you're ready to cook the doughnuts, in a deep fryer, heavy saucepan or deep skillet, heat at least 1 inch of oil to 365°F.

6. Working in small batches, fry the doughnuts for 1 minute or until golden brown on each side. Remove from the oil with tongs and drain well on paper towels.

7. Mix together the confectioners' sugar and cinnamon. Dust liberally on the doughnuts.

NOTEBOOK

BAKER'S

Granulated yeast comes packed in little envelopes and is easier to use than fresh, or cake, yeast, but fresh cake yeast is preferable. It has a wonderful "yeasty" flavor that many bread lovers crave. At any rate, both are living substances and must be proofed to jump-start the fermentation process and ensure that they are alive and kicking. To proof, just dissolve with a little sugar and/or flour in a liquid that is approximately 98–110°F. (like we do in step 2 above). It should bubble up within 15 minutes.

Depending on the humidity, flour in your cupboard can absorb surprisingly large amounts of moisture from the air. So, as the humidity changes, the amount of flour required in the recipe can actually change also. All recipes for yeast doughs in this book will start out with the smallest amount of flour possibly needed. You may have to add more until you achieve the consistency that the recipe calls for.

jelly DOUGHNUTS

When I was in college, we were sometimes able to score unfilled jelly doughnuts from a local doughnut shop, and we filled them with imported French preserves. What a treat . . . when we were lucky. One baker was accommodating but the other always refused our request. There is a much more dependable way to guarantee your choice of filling and that's to make your own doughnuts and fill them as you please.

For an added treat, you could also liberally dust the doughnuts with confectioners' sugar or coat them with Cinnamon Sugar (page 173).

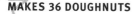 **MAKES 36 DOUGHNUTS**

Yeast Doughnuts (page 176)
1 cup of your favorite preserves: seedless raspberry, strawberry, blueberry,
    peach, apple, apricot, etc.

1. With a paring knife, pierce the side of a doughnut three-fourths of the way through. Carefully wriggle the knife back and forth to cut a small cavity in the doughnut's interior.

2. Fill a pastry bag with a ½-inch plain tip. Fill the bag a third full of jam (if you fill it too much, it will just ooze out the back and make a big mess).

3. Insert the pastry tip into the slit as far as you can get it without ripping the doughnut. Squeeze in a tablespoon or two of jam. Repeat with the rest of the doughnuts.

BAKER'S NOTEBOOK

Since the jam or preserves must be piped through a small pastry tip, they should be as smooth as possible. If they are chunky, purée them in a food processor. If they are very thick, vigorously stir in a tablespoon or two of water. In any case, giving that jam a good stir will loosen it up and make piping a whole lot smoother.

VARIATIONS

CREAM-FILLED DOUGHNUTS Follow the above instructions for Jelly Doughnuts, substituting a half-recipe of Vanilla Pudding (page 36) for the jelly filling. Leave plain or frost with Chocolate Glaze (page 180).

CHOCOLATE-FILLED DOUGHNUTS Follow the above instructions for Jelly Doughnuts, substituting a half-recipe of Chocolate Pudding (page 77) for the jelly filling. Leave plain or frost with Chocolate Glaze (page 180).

CHOCOLATE glazed doughnuts

When my elder daughter was two, she pointed out that for a pastry to legitimately be called "cake" it had to be doughnut-shaped, liberally frosted with chocolate and generously coated in multicolored sprinkles. Well, you can' t argue with logic. Enhance any of the doughnuts on the preceding or following pages with a shiny chocolate glaze. Your inner toddler will just love it.

MAKES A LITTLE MORE THAN 1 CUP OF GLAZE, ENOUGH FOR 24 DOUGHNUTS

CHOCOLATE GLAZE
3 tablespoons strong brewed coffee
2 tablespoons light corn syrup
$\frac{1}{2}$ cup sugar
4 ounces chopped semisweet or bittersweet chocolate

1 batch of doughnuts, any variety
Multicolored sprinkles (optional)

1. Make the Chocolate Glaze: In a small saucepan, heat the coffee, corn syrup and sugar over high heat until the sugar dissolves completely.

2. Put the chocolate in a medium bowl and pour the hot syrup over it. Gently stir until the chocolate is melted and smooth.

3. While the glaze is still hot, drag the doughnuts through so that one side is coated. Let the excess drip back into the bowl. If you choose, immediately coat with sprinkles. Place on a wire rack to set, about 15 minutes.

FUNNEL cakes

Whether it's a carnival, county fair or a festival, the longest lines always lead to the wildest rides and the funnel cakes. The perfect funnel cake is crunchy, tender and still warm from the fryer. It should always be generously doused with sugar. Funnel cakes are a cinch to prepare and just as much fun to make at home.

SERVES 6 TO 8

2 cups all-purpose flour
$3/4$ teaspoon baking powder
$1/4$ teaspoon salt
2 large eggs
4 tablespoons unsalted butter, melted
Vegetable oil, preferably canola, for frying
Confectioners' sugar, for dusting

1. In a mixing bowl, stir together the flour, baking powder and salt. Make a well in the center and put the eggs in with $1\frac{1}{2}$ cups of water. Mix the liquids into the flour, then mix in the melted butter.

2. Pour the batter into a pastry bag fitted with a $\frac{1}{4}$-inch plain tip.

3. Meanwhile, in a deep fryer, heavy saucepan or deep skillet, heat at least $1\frac{1}{2}$ inches of oil to 365°F.

4. Pipe out a $\frac{1}{4}$-cup squiggle of batter into the oil. When the underside is golden brown, turn it with tongs. When the second side browns, lift it out with the tongs and drain on paper towels. Repeat with the rest of the batter.

5. Dust liberally with confectioners' sugar.

NOTEBOOK

BAKER'S

You may also push the batter through a funnel and into the oil. Be careful. This way is a little trickier than the pastry bag method and the oil may splatter.

apple FRITTERS

Fried, fruit-filled fritters and dumplings are a yummy tradition from Central and Eastern Europe. Simple recipes like this one were brought here by immigrants in the nineteenth and early twentieth centuries. Today, fritters, usually filled with chopped apples, can be found in doughnut shops across America. The batter for these fruity, crunchy gems has to rest for at least 2 hours, so plan accordingly.

SERVES 6

$1\frac{1}{4}$ cups all-purpose flour plus about $\frac{1}{2}$ cup more for dredging

1 tablespoon melted butter

2 large eggs, separated

1 cup flat beer

$\frac{1}{4}$ teaspoon salt

Pinch of cream of tartar

1 tablespoon granulated sugar

1 teaspoon baking powder

2 Granny Smith apples, peeled, cored and cut into $\frac{1}{4}$-inch-thick rings

Vegetable oil, preferably canola, for frying

$\frac{1}{4}$ cup confectioners' sugar

$\frac{1}{2}$ teaspoon ground cinnamon

Brown Sugar Custard Sauce (page 246)

1. In a mixing bowl, stir together the $1\frac{1}{4}$ cups flour, butter, and egg yolks. Gradually stir in the beer. Set aside in the refrigerator for at least 2 hours, but preferably overnight (up to 12 hours).

2. Once the egg yolk mixture has rested, in a clean, dry mixing bowl, whisk the egg whites with the salt and cream of tartar until creamy and foamy. While still whisking (of course, you can use an electric mixer) sprinkle in the sugar and baking powder. Whisk until the egg whites hold firm peaks and are the consistency of shaving cream.

3. Fold the egg whites into the egg yolk mixture a third at a time to form the batter.

4. In a deep fryer, heavy saucepan or deep skillet, heat ¾ inch of oil to 365°F.

5. Set the bowl of batter near the fryer, alongside a shallow bowl filled with the ½ cup of flour for dredging. Dredge individual rings of apple, coating lightly. Dip into the batter to completely coat.

6. Working in small batches, fry the fritters for 3 minutes on each side, or until golden brown. Remove from the oil with tongs and drain well on paper towels.

7. Mix together the confectioners' sugar and cinnamon and dust it liberally on the fritters. Serve while still hot with Brown Sugar Custard Sauce.

VARIATION

Try substituting pear, banana, mango or papaya for the apple.

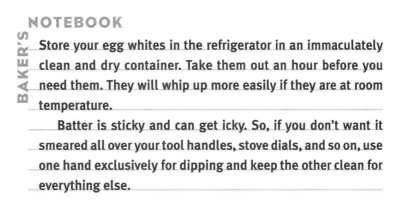

NOTEBOOK

BAKER'S

Store your egg whites in the refrigerator in an immaculately clean and dry container. Take them out an hour before you need them. They will whip up more easily if they are at room temperature.

Batter is sticky and can get icky. So, if you don't want it smeared all over your tool handles, stove dials, and so on, use one hand exclusively for dipping and keep the other clean for everything else.

Toll House Style Chocolate Chip Cookies ★ Oatmeal Cookies with Walnuts & Chocolate Chips ★ Chewy Chocolate-Oatmeal Cookies with Peanuts ★ Pineapple, Macadamia & White Chocolate Chunk Droppers ★ Cashew Fudge Drops ★ Peanut Butter Sandies ★ Benne Wafers ★ Gingerbread Persons ★ Oatmeal Raisin Cookies ★ Molasses "Cry Baby" Lace Cookies ★ Pecan-Graham Drop Cookies ★ Bourbon Snaps ★ Nutty Butterballs ★ Chocolate Butterballs ★ Blondies ★ Super Fudge Brownies ★ Lemon Bars with Pecan Crust ★ Coconut Bars ★ Chocolate-Coconut Bars ★ Whoopie Pies ★ Chocolate-filled Peanut Butter & Jelly Sandwich Cookies ★ Shortnin' Bread ★ Nebraska Lemon, Cornmeal & Pecan Shortbread ★ Chocolate-Peanut Biscotti

cookies, brownies & bars

Cookies hold a very special place in the hearts and souls of Americans. Like their French and English predecessors, they were originally referred to as biscuits but somewhere along the way adapted a form of their Dutch name, *kookje*. Most importantly, American cookies shed the restrained, one-dimensional tastes and textures of their European ancestors. They are completely indulgent and crammed full of flavor, and they come in countless permutations. They can be made with chunks and chips of chocolate, all sorts of nuts, dried fruits, grains and spices, or any combination of the above. There are three categories of cookie that are particularly American:

DROP COOKIES, like chocolate chip, are made with a soft dough that just gets "dropped" out onto the cookie sheet. Closely related are rolled cookies (those cut into shapes with cutters) and icebox cookies, which are chilled in a cylinder and sliced before baking.

BAR COOKIES are baked to a chewy consistency in a square or rectangular pan. Popular examples are brownies, blondies and lemon bars.

SANDWICH COOKIES consist of two cookies stuffed with a creamy filling to form a sandwich.

TIPS

When baking cookies, remember the most important rule: They must all contain a knockout punch of big-time yummy, whether it be chocolate, nuts, fruit or even bourbon.

Here are some more tips:

★ Try using a small ice cream scoop to form evenly sized drop cookies.

★ Don't just plop cookie dough all over the cookie sheet. Arrange your cookies in an orderly fashion. Staggered lines will conserve room and help prevent cookies from merging with each other as they spread. (Bakers call this process marrying.)

★ If the dough is too sticky, try rolling it between sheets of waxed paper.

★ Let cookies cool right on the sheets set on a rack. If you try to move the cookies to racks when they're hot, they'll just scrunch up.

★ Always allow cookie pans to cool before reusing. If the cookie sheet or the dough are too warm, the butter can melt out before the cookies set in the oven. To retain their shape, rolled cookies should start out chilled.

★ Remember that a timer is just a signal to check your cookies' progress and not a guarantee that they're done. Halfway through baking, turn your pans back to front for even baking.

★ Unless it is specified otherwise in the directions, don't try to remove cookies from the cookie sheet until they are somewhat cooled and set.

★ Feel free to change the size of your cookies. Make them bigger, smaller or in different shapes. Just keep an eye on how they are doing in the oven, as you may need to adjust the baking time.

TOLL HOUSE STYLE
chocolate chip cookies

These most classic of American cookies were first created by Ruth Wakefield, owner of the Toll House Inn, in Whitman, Massachusetts. Now back then, they didn't have chips or morsels, so Ruth chopped up bars of Nestlé semisweet chocolate and mixed it into a cookie batter. When the recipe appeared in a Boston newspaper, sales for the chocolate bars skyrocketed. Nestlé brokered a deal with Ruth that got them the name and recipe while she got a lifetime supply of chocolate. In 1939, the Nestlé company started making and selling packaged chocolate morsels. Here is an easy but extremely tasty version of Ruth's cookie gems.

MAKES 60 COOKIES

2¼ cups all-purpose flour

1 teaspoon baking soda

¾ teaspoon salt

1 cup (2 sticks) unsalted butter, at room temperature

¾ cup granulated sugar

1 cup lightly packed light brown sugar

2 large eggs

2 teaspoons vanilla extract

1 tablespoon dark rum

12 ounces semisweet chocolate morsels

1½ cups lightly toasted walnuts or pecans (see page 10), coarsely chopped

1. Preheat the oven to 375°F., arranging racks in the middle and top positions.

2. In a medium bowl, stir together the flour, baking soda, and salt and set aside.

3. Using an electric mixer, beat the butter, granulated sugar and brown sugar on medium speed in a large bowl for 15 seconds, until blended. Beat in the eggs until smooth, about 30 seconds more, then beat in the vanilla and rum. With the mixer on its lowest setting, gradually add the flour mixture, blending just to combine. Mix in the chocolate morsels and nuts.

4. Place tablespoons of dough onto nonstick or parchment-lined cookie sheets at 3-inch intervals. With moistened fingers, flatten and round out the dough balls a little. Bake at 375°F. for 12 minutes, or until the cookies are evenly browned, turning the cookie sheet around midway through baking. Set the cookies, sheet and all, on a rack to cool.

VARIATION

TRILLION-CHIP TOLL HOUSE COOKIES For an ultra jolt of chocolate, increase the chip population of your Toll House Style cookies. Follow the above recipe, but increase the amount of chocolate morsels to 18 ounces. Mix approximately 12 ounces into the batter as usual. Put the remaining 6 ounces in a small bowl. As you form the cookies into balls, press them into the morsels and flatten a little. Flip them over onto the cookie sheet (morsel side up) and bake as usual.

OATMEAL COOKIES
with walnuts & chocolate chips

Since its inception as Fort Snelling, Minneapolis has been a focal point of American wheat production. Today it is the home of the Grain Exchange, the international trading house for options and futures of grainy commodities. Add some of the state's famous butter, then some sugar from more than 16,000 of the area's sugar beet growers, and you're on your way to filling your shopping list for these cookies.

Even the concept of using maple syrup as a flavoring has Twin City roots. Patrick Towle, a St. Paul grocer, came up with the idea of blending real maple syrup with simple sugar syrup to make an affordable topping for pancakes. Since then, maple has become a favorite American flavoring and sweetener.

MAKES 30 COOKIES

1 cup all-purpose flour

$^1/_2$ teaspoon baking powder

$^1/_2$ teaspoon baking soda

$^1/_4$ teaspoon salt

2 cups old-fashioned rolled oats

$^1/_2$ cup lightly toasted walnuts (see page 10), coarsely chopped

$^1/_2$ cup (1 stick) unsalted butter, at room temperature

$^1/_2$ cup lightly packed light brown sugar

$^1/_2$ cup granulated sugar

1 large egg

$^1/_4$ cup pure maple syrup

4 ounces ($^2/_3$ cup) semisweet chocolate morsels

1. Preheat the oven to 350°F., arranging racks in the middle and upper positions.

2. In a medium bowl, stir the flour, baking powder, baking soda, salt, oats and walnuts together with a whisk or fork and set aside.

3. Using an electric mixer, beat the butter, brown sugar and granulated sugar on medium speed in a large bowl for 15 seconds, or until just blended. Beat in the egg until smooth, about 30 seconds more. With the mixer on medium speed, drizzle in the maple syrup until incorporated. Turn the mixer down to its lowest setting and gradually add the flour-oatmeal mixture, blending just to combine. Mix in the chocolate morsels.

4. Place walnut-size balls of dough onto nonstick or parchment-lined cookie sheets at 3-inch intervals. With moistened fingers, flatten and round out the dough balls a little. Bake at 350°F. for 12 minutes, or until the cookies are lightly browned on top, turning the cookie sheet around midway through baking. Set the cookies, sheet and all, on a rack to cool.

CHEWY CHOCOLATE-
oatmeal cookies with peanuts

For years we have heard that just about anything that we liked was bad for us. Now, as it turns out, many things that were supposed to be bad are surprisingly good for us. Case in point: chocolate. Throw in some oatmeal and you have the makings of a cookie that any health nut would approve of. And speaking of nuts, let's add a whole bunch. Peanuts that is. These cookies spread thin, resulting in a crunchy outside and a chewy, chewy inside, so leave enough room between them on your cookie sheet.

MAKES 40 COOKIES

8 ounces (1⅓ cups) semisweet chocolate morsels
¾ cup all-purpose flour
¼ teaspoon baking powder
¼ teaspoon baking soda
¼ teaspoon salt
1½ cups old-fashioned rolled oats
¾ cup unsalted, roasted peanuts, coarsely chopped
½ cup (1 stick) unsalted butter, at room temperature
1 cup granulated sugar
1 large egg
¼ cup pure maple syrup

1. Preheat the oven to 375°F., arranging racks in the middle and upper positions.

2. Melt half of the chocolate morsels in a completely dry bowl or double boiler set over barely simmering water.

3. In a medium bowl, stir the flour, baking powder, baking soda, salt, oats and peanuts together with a whisk or fork. Set aside.

4. Using an electric mixer, beat the butter and sugar on medium speed for 15 seconds, or until blended. Beat in the egg until smooth, about 30 seconds more. With the mixer on medium speed, drizzle in the maple syrup to incorporate. Turn the mixer down to its lowest setting and gradually add the flour-oatmeal mixture. Mix in the melted chocolate until blended, then mix in the remaining chocolate chips.

5. Place rounded tablespoons of dough onto nonstick or parchment-lined cookie sheets at 3-inch intervals. With moistened fingers, round out and flatten the dough balls a little. Bake at 375°F. for 12 minutes, or until the cookies are lightly browned on the edges, turning the cookie sheets around midway through baking. Set the cookies, sheet and all, on a rack to cool.

NOTEBOOK

BAKER'S For that chewy oatmeal texture, make sure to use old-fashioned-style oats, and not quick or instant oats.

Early Midwestern pioneers used dog-powered treadmills to churn butter. They also used woof-powered bean threshers.

PINEAPPLE, MACADAMIA & white chocolate chunk droppers

How much more exotic could you get than the rich and rare macadamia? How about the combination of these rich Hawaiian nuts with white chocolate? In the late '80s and early '90s, this combination was all the rage at cookie shops across the mainland. To make these chippers even more sensual, I've added succulent dried pineapple. Today, widespread cultivation around the globe has made macadamia nuts more available but, to tell you the truth, the imported versions are not as good as the domestic Hawaiian originals.

MAKES 36 COOKIES

2 rings of dried pineapple cut into ⅓-inch chunks (about 1 cup, or 3½ ounces)

1¼ cups all-purpose flour

¾ teaspoon baking powder

¼ teaspoon baking soda

¼ teaspoon salt

½ cup (1 stick) unsalted butter, at room temperature

½ cup granulated sugar

¾ cup lightly packed light brown sugar

1 large egg

2 tablespoons dark rum

¾ cup (4 ounces) unsalted macadamia nuts, very coarsely chopped

4 ounces (¾ cup) white chocolate morsels

1. Preheat the oven to 350°F., arranging racks in the middle and top positions.

2. In a small saucepan, barely cover the pineapple chunks with water and bring to a boil. Remove from heat and let soak for 5 minutes. Drain well.

3. In a medium bowl, stir together the flour, baking powder, baking soda and salt and set aside.

4. Using an electric mixer, beat the butter, granulated sugar and brown sugar on medium speed for 15 seconds, or until blended. Beat in the egg until smooth, about 30 seconds more. Beat in the rum. With the mixer on its lowest setting, gradually add the flour mixture, blending just to combine. Mix in the macadamia nuts and white chocolate morsels. Mix in the drained pineapple.

5. Place rounded tablespoons of dough onto nonstick or parchment-lined cookie sheets at 3-inch intervals. With moistened fingers, flatten and round out the dough balls a little. Bake at 350°F. for 12 minutes, or until the cookies are evenly browned, turning the cookie sheets around midway through baking. Set the cookies, sheet and all, on a rack to cool.

NOTEBOOK

BAKER'S

When it comes to white chocolate, don't skimp on quality. Good white chocolate is expensive and the cheap stuff is usually not very good. Make sure you buy white chocolate that contains cocoa butter and not vegetable shortening.

CASHEW FUDGE drops

If you are an incurable chocoholic and nuts for nuts, then these are the cookies that will drive you bonkers. They are fudgy to the extreme, studded with chocolate chips and chock-full of those most voluptuous of nuts, cashews.

MAKES 30 COOKIES

7 ounces (about 1¼ cups) semisweet chocolate morsels or chunks

1½ cups all-purpose flour

1 teaspoon baking powder

¼ teaspoon salt

1 cup roasted, unsalted cashews, chopped into big chunks

¾ cup (1½ sticks) unsalted butter, at room temperature

¼ cup granulated sugar

1 large egg

1. Preheat the oven to 375°F., arranging racks in the middle and upper positions.

2. Melt ½ cup of the chocolate morsels in a completely dry bowl or double boiler set over barely simmering water, then set aside.

3. In a medium bowl, stir the flour, baking powder, salt and cashews together with a whisk or fork and set aside.

4. Using an electric mixer, beat the butter and sugar on medium speed for 15 seconds, or until blended. Beat in the egg until smooth and barely fluffy, about 30 seconds more. Turn the mixer down to its lowest setting and gradually add the flour mixture. Mix in the melted chocolate until blended, then mix in the remaining chocolate chips.

5. Place rounded tablespoons of dough onto nonstick or parchment-lined cookie sheets at 3-inch intervals. With moistened fingers, flatten and round out the dough balls a little. Bake for 12 minutes, turning the cookie sheets around midway through baking. The cookies should look set but not darkened around the edges. Set the cookies, sheet and all, on a rack to cool.

peanut butter SANDIES

Early Colonial farmers in Georgia found peanuts, brought to America by African slaves, growing in their fields, but considered them fit only for pigs. Dr. George Washington Carver invented more than 300 uses for peanuts, from soup to ice cream. Now they are an important crop in that state and a staple of these cookie jar faves. Peanut Butter Sandies are tender, crumbly gems: studded with roasted peanuts and full of peanut butter flavor.

MAKES 30 COOKIES

1$\frac{1}{2}$ cups all-purpose flour

$\frac{3}{4}$ teaspoon baking soda

$\frac{1}{4}$ teaspoon salt

$\frac{1}{2}$ cup (1 stick) unsalted butter, at room temperature

$\frac{1}{4}$ cup lightly packed dark brown sugar

$\frac{3}{4}$ cup granulated sugar

1 cup smooth peanut butter

1 large egg

$\frac{1}{2}$ teaspoon vanilla extract

1 cup unsalted, roasted peanuts, coarsely chopped

1. Preheat the oven to 375°F., arranging racks in the middle and upper positions.

2. In a medium bowl, stir together the flour, baking soda and salt. Set aside.

3. Using an electric mixer, beat the butter, brown sugar and granulated sugar on medium speed for 15 seconds, or until blended. Beat in the peanut butter and then the egg until completely blended and smooth, about 30 seconds more. Beat in the vanilla. With the mixer on its lowest setting, gradually add the flour mixture, blending just to combine.

4. Put the chopped peanuts in a small bowl. Form the dough into walnut-size balls and dunk their tops into the peanuts. Flatten and round the dough balls out a little, then place them, nut side up, on nonstick or parchment-lined cookie sheets at 2$\frac{1}{2}$-inch intervals. Bake for 13 minutes, or until the cookies are just set and lightly tanned, turning the cookie sheets around midway through baking. Set the cookies, sheet and all, on a rack to cool.

BENNE wafers

Cookies, cakes and candies packed with toasted sesame seeds have been popular in the Carolinas since Colonial times. Their nutty, toasty flavor is just sensational. This recipe uses a little dark Asian sesame oil to enhance that deep sesame flavor.

MAKES ABOUT 60 COOKIES

1 cup raw sesame seeds

½ cup all-purpose flour

¼ teaspoon baking powder

¼ teaspoon salt

4 tablespoons unsalted butter, at room temperature

½ cup granulated sugar

¼ cup lightly packed dark brown sugar

1 large egg

2 tablespoons dark sesame oil

1 teaspoon vanilla extract

1. Preheat the oven to 350°F., arranging racks in the middle and upper positions.

2. Warm a large skillet over medium heat for 2 minutes. Cook the sesame seeds, stirring constantly, until light golden brown and fragrant. Remove the seeds from the pan and set aside to cool.

3. In a medium bowl, stir the flour, baking powder, and salt together with a whisk or fork. Set aside.

4. Using an electric mixer, beat the butter, granulated sugar and brown sugar together for 15 seconds, or until blended. Beat in the egg until smooth, about 30 seconds more. With the mixer on medium speed, drizzle in the oil until incorporated. Turn the mixer to its lowest setting and add the vanilla. Gradually add the flour mixture, then the sesame seeds.

5. Place rounded teaspoons of dough onto nonstick or parchment-lined cookie sheets at 2½-inch intervals. Bake at 350°F. for 9 minutes, or until the cookies have spread out and turned a golden tan, turning the cookie sheets around midway through baking. Set the cookies, sheet and all, on a rack to cool.

GINGERBREAD persons

Unfortunately, as adorable as they look, gingerbread men, women and houses usually taste no better than plasterboard. Here is the exception—these little fellers and gals are so full of delicious flavor they don' t even need to be decorated.

MAKES ABOUT 24 COOKIES

2 cups all-purpose flour

1 tablespoon ground ginger

1 teaspoon ground cinnamon

$\frac{1}{2}$ teaspoon ground cloves

$\frac{1}{2}$ teaspoon baking soda

$\frac{1}{4}$ teaspoon salt

$\frac{1}{2}$ cup (1 stick) unsalted butter, at room temperature

$\frac{1}{2}$ cup sugar

1 egg

$\frac{1}{4}$ cup molasses

1 teaspoon vanilla extract

1 teaspoon orange extract or orange liqueur such as Grand Marnier

1. Preheat the oven to 350°F., arranging the rack in the middle position.

2. In a medium bowl, stir together the flour, ginger, cinnamon, cloves, baking soda and salt. In the bowl of an electric mixer, beat the butter and sugar together on medium speed for 15 seconds, or until smooth. Beat in the egg until completely blended, about 30 seconds. Beat in the molasses, vanilla and orange extract. Turn the mixer down to its lowest speed and gradually add the flour and spice mixture, blending just to combine.

3. Roll the dough out between two sheets of wax paper to a $\frac{1}{4}$-inch thickness. Refrigerate on a flat surface for 30 minutes until firm. With a 3-inch person-shaped cookie cutter, cut out shapes and transfer to a nonstick or parchment-lined cookie sheet. Refrigerate for 15 minutes (to help the cookies hold their shape while baking). Gather the remaining scraps of dough into a ball, roll it out, chill the dough until firm again, and cut out more cookies.

4. Bake the cookies for 12 minutes, turning the sheet midway through baking, until lightly tanned around the edges. Set the cookies, sheet and all, on a rack to cool.

oatmeal raisin COOKIES

Oatmeal cookies are the most homespun of American cookies: chewy and nourishing. These are crisp on the outside and soft at the center. In many places they are called rocks, a reference to their craggy outer texture. On the West Coast they are sometimes made with dates and called Billy Goats. If that is your preference, just substitute a cup of chopped, pitted dates for the raisins.

MAKES 30 COOKIES

1 cup raisins
1 cup all-purpose flour
$\frac{1}{2}$ teaspoon baking powder
$\frac{1}{2}$ teaspoon baking soda
$\frac{1}{2}$ teaspoon salt
1 teaspoon ground cinnamon
2 cups old-fashioned rolled oats
1 cup lightly packed light brown sugar
1 cup lightly toasted walnuts (see page 10), coarsely chopped
$\frac{1}{2}$ cup (1 stick) unsalted butter, at room temperature
1 large egg
$\frac{1}{2}$ cup pure maple syrup
1 teaspoon vanilla extract

1. In a small saucepan, cover the raisins with water and bring to a simmer. Remove from the heat and let sit for 10 minutes.

2. Preheat the oven to 375°F., arranging a rack in the middle position.

3. Using an electric mixer on its lowest setting, mix together the flour, baking powder, baking soda, salt, cinnamon, oatmeal, brown sugar and walnuts. Continuing to beat, add the butter, then the egg, maple syrup and vanilla. Mix until the dough is thoroughly blended and massed together. Drain the raisins and mix in.

4. Place walnut-size balls of dough on nonstick or parchment-lined cookie sheets at 3-inch intervals. Bake at 375°F. for 18 minutes, or until lightly browned, turning the cookie sheets around midway through baking. Set the cookies, sheet and all, on a rack to cool.

MOLASSES "cry baby" LACE COOKIES

To quiet down squawking children, pioneers of the Virginia Piedmont region baked molasses cookies, aptly named cry babies. Inspired by those cry babies, these deep, smoky lace cookies have crisp centers and an almost candylike crunch around the edges. Back in the old days, cookies like these might have been made with hickory nuts. Today, it's hard to find them and even harder to pry the meat out of them, but hazelnuts are easy to find and taste even better.

MAKES 30 COOKIES

$\frac{1}{2}$ cup plus 2 tablespoons ($1\frac{1}{4}$ sticks) unsalted butter, melted

$\frac{1}{4}$ cup granulated sugar

$\frac{1}{2}$ cup dark corn syrup

2 tablespoons unsulphured molasses (such as Grandma's Mild brand)

1 cup all-purpose flour

$\frac{1}{2}$ cup skinned, roasted hazelnuts, finely chopped

1. Preheat the oven to 350°F., arranging a rack in the middle position.

2. In a small saucepan, bring the butter, sugar, corn syrup and molasses to a simmer over medium heat, stirring to prevent scorching. Remove from the heat and stir in the flour and nuts.

3. Working in batches of no more than 6, drop scant tablespoons of dough on a nonstick or well-greased cookie sheet at 4-inch intervals. Bake at 350°F. for 5 minutes, until the cookies are the color of coffee with a little bit of milk in it and bubbling. Remove the cookies from the oven and let cool for 3 minutes.

4. While the cookies are still hot, but firm enough to move, lift them up with a spatula and drape them over a rolling pin, glass bottle or banana. Let set and continue with the rest of the batter. As the cookies turn crisp, slide them off their molds and reuse the bottles or rolling pin. If you want to keep them flat, just let them cool on the cookie sheet.

PECAN-GRAHAM drop cookies

For those of you who think that today's whole foods movement is a holdout from the granola-crunching Sixties, guess again. In the early 1800s, an influential advocate of whole grains was Sylvester Graham of Northampton, Massachusetts. His healthy namesake crackers became "ingrained" in American baking. Generations later, with only the yummy factor in mind, American Girl Scouts started making s'mores—graham cracker sandwiches with toasted marshmallows and chocolate. Here is a pecan drop cookie that is based on Sylvester's original formula for the graham cracker. It is made with all of the wholesome ingredients that he recommended. It would thrill any Boy or Girl Scout and would probably make Old Doc Graham proud, also.

MAKES 36 COOKIES

¾ cup (about 3 ounces) lightly toasted pecans (see page 10),
    finely chopped
1¼ cups whole wheat flour
½ cup rye flour
1½ teaspoons baking powder
1 teaspoon baking soda
1 teaspoon ground cinnamon
½ teaspoon salt
½ cup (1 stick) unsalted butter, at room temperature
1 cup granulated sugar
1 large egg
1 tablespoon unsulphured molasses
1 tablespoon honey
½ teaspoon vanilla extract

1. Preheat the oven to 375°F., arranging racks in the middle and top positions.

2. In a medium bowl, stir together the pecans, the whole wheat and rye flours, baking powder, baking soda, cinnamon and salt and set aside.

3. Using an electric mixer, beat the butter and sugar on medium speed for 15 seconds, or until just blended. Add the egg and beat for 30 seconds, or until smooth. With the mixer on its lowest setting, beat in half of the flour mixture, blending just to combine. Add the molasses, honey and vanilla, then beat in the rest of the flour mixture.

4. Place rounded tablespoons of dough onto nonstick or parchment-lined cookie sheets at 2½-inch intervals. With moistened fingers, flatten and round the dough balls out a little. Bake at 375°F. for about 12 minutes, turning the cookie sheets around midway through baking. Set the cookies, sheet and all, on a rack to cool.

Hard tack, a prototype of the cracker, was once eaten by sailors on long voyages. A sea captain named Joshua Bent came up with a light version and called them (quite onomatopoetically) "crackers." They were so good that they became a hit on land. They soon had competition from the newly established Kennedy Biscuit Company in Newton, Massachusetts, where, yes the Fig Newton would be invented. The two family businesses eventually went on to collaborate together and play a major part in the formation of the National Biscuit Company (now known as Nabisco). In 1898, they developed the Ritz cracker, and in 1902, Barnum's Animal Crackers.

bourbon SNAPS

These elegant cylinder-shape cookies were adapted from British brandy snaps. These dainty, whipped-cream-filled gems were the stars of antebellum plantations, where they were stacked in pyramids to impress dinner guests.

MAKES 24 COOKIES

Nonstick vegetable-oil spray
$\frac{1}{2}$ cup (1 stick) unsalted butter
$\frac{1}{2}$ cup lightly packed light brown sugar
$\frac{1}{2}$ cup dark corn syrup
1 cup all-purpose flour
1 teaspoon ground cinnamon
1 tablespoon bourbon

BOURBON WHIPPED CREAM
1 cup heavy or whipping cream
$\frac{1}{4}$ cup confectioners' sugar
1 tablespoon bourbon
$\frac{1}{2}$ teaspoon vanilla extract

1. Preheat the oven to 350°F., arranging racks in the middle and upper positions. Coat the handles of several wooden mixing spoons with nonstick vegetable-oil spray.

2. In a small saucepan, bring the butter, brown sugar and corn syrup to a simmer over medium heat, stirring to prevent scorching. Remove from heat and stir in the flour, cinnamon and bourbon.

3. Working in batches of no more than 5 cookies per cookie sheet, drop rounded teaspoons of dough on 2 nonstick or well-greased cookie sheets at 3½-inch intervals. Bake at 350°F. for 6 minutes, until the cookies are golden, spread out and bubbly, exchanging the cookie sheets midway through baking. Remove the cookie sheets from the oven and let cool for 1 minute.

4. When just barely firm enough to handle, carefully lift a cookie off with a spatula and wrap it around a spoon handle to form a $3/4$-inch-wide tube. Let set and continue with the rest. As the cookies harden, slide them off the spoon handles and wrap another cookie. Continue with the rest of the batter, baking, cooling and shaping.

5. Make the Bourbon Whipped Cream: In a chilled bowl, whip the cream until slightly thickened. Add the confectioners' sugar, bourbon and vanilla. Whip to the consistency of shaving cream. Chill until you're ready to serve the cookies.

6. To serve the cookies, put the whipped cream into a pastry bag fitted with a $1/2$-inch plain tip and pipe it into the cookie tubes.

nutty BUTTERBALLS

They pop up all over the world with names like Mexican Wedding Cakes, Swedish Christmas Cookies or Meltaways. Wherever they come from, these crumbly, tender butter cookies have long been naturalized citizens of the United States. These cookies are coated with confectioners' sugar twice, once while still hot so that the sugar melts into a sticky frosting, and again when cooled to give them a powdery coating.

MAKES ABOUT 30 COOKIES

1 cup lightly toasted pecans or walnuts (see page 10), finely chopped

2 cups all-purpose flour

$3/4$ cup confectioners' sugar, plus about $1/4$ cup more for sprinkling

$3/4$ cup ($1 1/2$ sticks) unsalted butter, at room temperature

1 large egg

1 teaspoon vanilla extract

1 tablespoon dark rum

1. Preheat the oven to 350°F., arranging racks in the middle and upper positions.

2. In a food processor fitted with the metal blade, or in the bowl of an electric mixer, mix together the nuts, flour and confectioners' sugar. While pulsing, or on low speed, add the butter, then the egg. Add the vanilla and rum. Process or beat until the dough is thoroughly blended and massed together.

3. Form rounded tablespoons of batter into balls. Place them on nonstick or parchment-lined cookie sheets at $1 1/2$-inch intervals. Refrigerate for 30 minutes, or until firm. Bake at 350°F. for 13 minutes, or until the cookies are lightly tanned around the edges and just set, turning the cookie sheets around midway through baking.

4. With a small strainer or dredge can, sprinkle a thin coating of confectioners' sugar on the hot cookies. Set the cookies, sheet and all, on a rack to cool. When completely cool, sprinkle on more confectioners' sugar.

BAKER'S NOTEBOOK

You may also form the batter into 30 crescent-shaped cookies.

HAZELNUT BUTTERBALLS Substitute blanched, skinned, roasted hazelnuts for the pecans or walnuts. Substitute 1 tablespoon hazelnut liqueur, such as Frangelico, for the rum and vanilla.

ALMOND BUTTERBALLS Substitute your choice of lightly toasted almonds (whole, slivered or sliced; with or without skins) for the pecans or walnuts. Substitute 1 tablespoon almond liqueur, such as Amaretto di Saronno, for the rum and vanilla.

MACADAMIA OR CASHEW BUTTERBALLS Substitute store-bought, preroasted macadamias or cashews for the pecans or walnuts. (Since macadamias and cashews have higher oil contents, it is very difficult to roast them at home.)

CHOCOLATE butterballs

Here's a chocolate variation on this buttery, crumbly theme.

MAKES 30 COOKIES

1 cup lightly toasted pecans or walnuts (see page 10), finely chopped

1½ cups all-purpose flour

½ cup unsweetened, Dutch-processed cocoa powder

¾ cup confectioners' sugar, plus approximately ¼ cup more for sprinkling

¾ cup (1½ sticks) unsalted butter, at room temperature

1 large egg

1. Preheat the oven to 375°F., arranging racks in the middle and upper positions.

2. In a food processor fitted with a metal blade, or in the bowl of an electric mixer, mix together the nuts, flour, cocoa and confectioners' sugar. While pulsing, or on low speed, add the butter, then the egg. Process or beat until the dough is thoroughly blended and massed together.

3. Form rounded tablespoons of batter into balls. Place them on nonstick or parchment-lined cookie sheets at 1½-inch intervals. Refrigerate for 30 minutes, or until firm. Bake at 375°F. for 13 minutes, or until the cookies are set, turning the cookie sheets around midway through baking.

4. With a small strainer or dredge can, sprinkle a thin coating of confectioners' sugar on the hot cookies. Set the cookies, sheet and all, on a rack to cool. When completely cool, sprinkle on more confectioners' sugar.

blondies

A good blondie needs to have a little something extra, otherwise it just couldn't compete with its superstar brunette sister. Here's a blondie that's just packed with extras: rum, pecans and lots of flavor. So watch out, brownie lovers—there's a new kid in town.

MAKES 12 SQUARES

Nonstick vegetable-oil spray
1 cup (2 sticks) unsalted butter, at room temperature
1 cup lightly packed light brown sugar
2 large eggs
$^3/_4$ cup dark corn syrup (such as Karo brand)
2 tablespoons dark rum
2 cups all-purpose flour
$^1/_2$ teaspoon baking powder
$^1/_4$ teaspoon salt
**1$^1/_2$ cups unsalted, preroasted macadamias or cashews, or 1 cup toasted pecans
   (see page 10)**

1. Preheat the oven to 350°F., arranging a rack in the middle position. Lightly coat a 13 × 9-inch nonstick baking pan with nonstick vegetable-oil spray.

2. In a large bowl, mix together the butter, sugar, eggs, corn syrup and rum until blended.

3. In a medium bowl, stir together the flour, baking powder, and salt. Mix it into the egg mixture. Stir in 1 cup of the nuts.

4. Spread in the prepared pan and sprinkle the remaining $^1/_2$ cup of the nuts on top. Bake at 350°F. for 25 minutes, or until crusty on top but just barely set. Set the pan on a rack to cool. Cut into 3-inch squares.

VARIATION

WHITE CHOCOLATE BLONDIES Mix 1 cup of white chocolate morsels or chunks into the batter.

super fudge BROWNIES

There are two types of brownies: the crumbly cake style and the chocolaty, rich and chewy fudge style. I imagine that someone, somewhere prefers a cakelike brownie, but I have yet to meet him. For the rest of us, here are the richest, chewiest, deepest, darkest and most sensual brownies ever.

The simple trick for creating a gooey brownie is to start with a good recipe (like this one, of course) and make sure that you don't overbake it. The brownies are done when the batter is just barely set.

MAKES 12 SQUARES

Nonstick vegetable-oil spray
1 pound bittersweet or semisweet chocolate (see Baker's Notebook)
³/₄ cup (1¹/₂ sticks) unsalted butter
4 large eggs
1 cup lightly packed light brown sugar
¹/₂ cup granulated sugar
2 teaspoons vanilla extract
1¹/₄ cups all-purpose flour
¹/₄ teaspoon baking powder
¹/₄ teaspoon salt
1¹/₂ cups lightly toasted walnuts (see page 10), coarsely chopped

1. Preheat the oven to 350°F., arranging a rack in the middle position. Lightly coat a 13 × 9-inch nonstick baking pan with nonstick vegetable-oil spray.

2. In a completely dry bowl or double boiler set over barely simmering water, melt the chocolate and butter, stirring occasionally.

3. In a large bowl, mix together the eggs, brown sugar, granulated sugar and vanilla until blended. Mix in the chocolate.

4. In a medium bowl, stir together the flour, baking powder, and salt. Gradually mix it into the chocolate and egg mixture. Stir in 1 cup of the walnuts.

5. Spread into the prepared pan and sprinkle the remaining ½ cup of the walnuts on top. Bake at 350°F. for 20 to 25 minutes, or until slightly crusty and lightly cracked on top, but barely set. Set the pan on a rack to cool.

6. Cut into 3-inch squares.

VARIATION

KITCHEN SINK BROWNIES Customize your brownies by throwing in just about anything but the kitchen sink. Try mini chocolate morsels, marshmallows, any kind of nuts, raisins or any other dried fruits. It's also fun to sprinkle ½ cup of chocolate morsels or chunks over the top before baking.

NOTEBOOK

BAKER'S

When it comes to chocolate, some like it bitter, some like it semisweet. It's all a matter of taste. If you are having trouble locating bittersweet chocolate, fabricate your own blend. Substitute 14 ounces of semisweet and 2 ounces of unsweetened for 1 pound of bittersweet.

The best way to cut brownies, and other bar cookies, is to invert the whole pan onto a cookie sheet, then flip it over onto a cutting board. You can now cut your brownies without scratching the interior of your brownie pan.

lemon bars
WITH PECAN CRUST

It's hard to find a "real" lemon bar with so many curd- or goo-topped impostors out there. Those aren't lemon bars, they're just slices of lemon tart or who-knows-what. These bars are the real McCoy. They are as lemony as sour balls and have a chewy, gumdrop-like texture. And check this out—the bottom crust is chock-full of crunchy pecans.

MAKES 12 SQUARES

PECAN CRUST
Nonstick vegetable-oil spray
1½ cups all-purpose flour
½ cup lightly toasted pecans (see page 10), finely chopped
¼ cup confectioners' sugar
¼ cup lightly packed light brown sugar
½ cup plus 2 tablespoons (1¼ sticks) unsalted butter, at room temperature

LEMON FILLING
1½ cups sugar
½ cup all-purpose flour
6 large eggs
Grated zest of 3 lemons (about 3 tablespoons)
1 cup fresh lemon juice (from about 6 lemons)
¾ teaspoon vanilla extract
Confectioners' sugar, for dusting

1. Make the Pecan Crust: Lightly coat a 13 × 9-inch baking pan with nonstick vegetable-oil spray. In a mixing bowl or food processor, mix together the flour, pecans, confectioners' sugar, brown sugar and butter until crumbly and the consistency of streusel. Pat it evenly over the bottom of the pan. With a fork, prick little holes in the dough. Refrigerate for 30 minutes, or until firm.

2. Preheat the oven to 375°F., arranging a rack in the middle position.

3. Bake at 375°F. for 12 minutes, or until very lightly tanned and set. Transfer to a rack to cool, and lower the oven temperature to 325°F.

4. Make the Lemon Filling: In a medium bowl, combine the sugar and flour. Beat in the eggs, then the lemon zest, juice and vanilla extract.

5. Pour the filling over the prebaked crust and bake at 325°F. for 15 minutes, or until set. Set the pan on a rack to cool. Cut into 3-inch squares. Dust liberally with confectioners' sugar.

NOTEBOOK

BAKER'S You will want a nice thick layer of lemon filling on your bars. If your baking pan is on the shallow side and might overflow, place it in the oven and then carefully pour in the lemon filling.

coconut **BARS**

Jews fleeing the Inquisition in Spain and Portugal were among the first Europeans to come to the New World. Many settled in Brazil but, after hearing of the religious freedoms offered in the Anglo-American colonies, migrated north. They brought with them a wonderful recipe for flourless coconut meringues called macaroons. These eventually turned into wonderful bar cookies, with a tender, crumbly crust and a top layer of moist macaroon. These bars are crispy and crusty on the outside but chewy and gooey in their interiors.

 **MAKES 12 SQUARES**

Nonstick vegetable-oil spray

COCONUT CRUST
³⁄₄ cup all-purpose flour
1 tablespoon granulated sugar
¹⁄₄ cup unsweetened shredded coconut (see Baker's Notebook)
5 tablespoons cold unsalted butter, cut into pea-size bits

COCONUT MACAROON
4 cups (12 ounces) unsweetened shredded coconut
8 large egg whites
2 cups confectioners' sugar
¹⁄₂ cup coconut cream (such as Coco López brand)

1. Lightly coat a 13 × 9-inch baking pan with nonstick vegetable-oil spray.

2. Make the Coconut Crust: In a bowl, stir together the flour, sugar and shredded coconut. With your fingertips or a pastry blender, work in the butter until the mixture looks like coarse meal. Sprinkle on 2 to 3 tablespoons of water and blend to mass the dough together. Pat or roll the dough out so it fits into the bottom of the baking pan. With a fork, prick little holes in the dough. Refrigerate while making the macaroon layer.

3. Preheat the oven to 375°F., arranging a rack in the middle position.

4. **Make the Coconut Macaroon:** In a large bowl, mix together the shredded coconut, egg whites, confectioners' sugar and coconut cream.

5. Lightly press this macaroon mixture over the coconut crust. Bake at 375°F. for 20 minutes, or until golden brown and just barely set. Transfer to a rack to cool.

6. Cut into 3-inch squares.

VARIATION

Don't feel locked into this crust recipe. You can also use Pecan Crust (page 212) or any leftover pie or tart dough.

BAKER'S NOTEBOOK Unsweetened, shredded coconut is available in specialty and health food stores and in Asian markets. It has much more flavor than the sweetened variety.

CHOCOLATE-COCONUT bars

In the early 1920s, Peter Paul Halajian, an Armenian immigrant, came up with a wonderful coconut bar enrobed in dark chocolate, which he called Mounds. In the 1940s he added two toasted almonds and a milk chocolate coating to produce the Almond Joy, which now out-sells Mounds bars 2 to 1. Today, the company that he founded goes through 50 million pounds of coconut from the Philippines every year. These baked coconut meringue bars have a crisp chocolate crust and a topping of rich chocolate truffle, all in tribute to Peter Paul's wonderful confection.

MAKES 12 SQUARES

Nonstick vegetable-oil spray

CHOCOLATE CRUST

1½ cups all-purpose flour

¼ cup granulated sugar

2 tablespoons unsweetened, Dutch-processed cocoa powder

½ cup (1 stick) unsalted butter, at room temperature

1 large egg

Coconut Macaroon (page 214), prepared according to step 4

Chocolate Truffle Drizzle (page 41)

½ cup whole almonds, lightly toasted (see page 10),
   coarsely chopped

1. Preheat the oven to 375°F., arranging a rack in the middle position. Lightly coat a 13 × 9-inch baking pan with nonstick vegetable-oil spray.

2. Make the Chocolate Crust: Put the flour, sugar and cocoa into the bowl of a food processor fitted with the metal blade. While pulsing, add the butter, bit by bit. Add the egg and process until the dough is thoroughly blended and masses together.

3. Between two sheets of waxed paper or parchment, roll the dough into a 9 × 13-inch rectangle. Peel off one sheet of the waxed paper and flip the dough into the bottom of the prepared baking pan. Peel off the other sheet. With a fork, prick little holes in the dough.

4. Lightly pat the coconut macaroon over the chocolate crust. Bake at 375°F. for 20 minutes, or until just golden brown and barely set. Set the pan on a rack to cool.

5. When cool, drizzle with Chocolate Truffle Drizzle. Sprinkle with the almonds. Let rest for 30 minutes, to set.

6. Cut into 3-inch squares.

Milton Hershey was not a success at first. He dropped out of his apprenticeship and failed in at least five business ventures involving candy before he returned home to Lancaster, Pennsylvania, with a new caramel recipe. When he couldn't get his caramel company off the ground, he decided to try his hand at chocolate making. Instead of developing a whole line of chocolate confections, he focused on one product—the Hershey bar. The rest is history.

whoopie PIES

The customs and cooking of America's tightly knit Amish communities have remained largely unaltered for over 200 years. So have many of the humorous names of their recipes: Funny Pie, Schnitz Pie, Shoofly Pie and, of course, the world-famous Whoopie Pie. These little cushions of chocolate, sandwiched around a vanilla cream center, are much softer than a cookie but firmer than a cake. The consistency is a lot like that of their big-city cousin and Jewish bakery favorite, the black & white cookie.

Although it wouldn't be considered all that kosher to use an electric mixer in Lancaster County, Pennsylvania, or other Amish enclaves, whoopie pies are much easier to make with modern appliances. So go ahead, crank up the KitchenAid, then "eat yourself full."

MAKES 24 SANDWICHES

COOKIES

1³⁄₄ cups all-purpose flour

³⁄₄ cup unsweetened, Dutch-processed cocoa powder

1 teaspoon baking powder

¹⁄₄ teaspoon salt

³⁄₄ cup (1¹⁄₂ sticks) unsalted butter, at room temperature

³⁄₄ cup granulated sugar

1 large egg

¹⁄₄ cup milk

1 tablespoon cider vinegar or lemon juice

¹⁄₂ cup strong brewed coffee

CREAMY VANILLA FILLING

¹⁄₄ cup vegetable shortening

4 tablespoons unsalted butter, at room temperature

1 cup confectioners' sugar

1 teaspoon vanilla extract

¹⁄₂ cup light corn syrup

1. Preheat the oven to 375°F., arranging racks in the middle and upper positions.

2. Sift the flour, cocoa, baking powder and salt together 3 times. Set aside.

3. Using an electric mixer, beat the butter and sugar together at high speed for 15 seconds, or until combined. Beat in the egg until blended, about 1 minute. With the mixer on its lowest setting, gradually add half of the flour mixture, blending just to combine. Beat in the milk, vinegar and coffee, then the rest of the flour mixture.

4. Place tablespoons of dough on nonstick or parchment-lined cookie sheets at $2^1/_2$-inch intervals. With moistened fingers, round out the dough balls and flatten them a little. Bake at 375°F. for 9 minutes, or until set, turning the cookie sheets around midway through baking. Set the cookie sheet on a rack to cool.

5. Make the Creamy Vanilla Filling: With an electric mixer, beat together the vegetable shortening and butter until blended. Turn the mixer down to its lowest setting and gradually add the confectioners' sugar. Turn the mixer back up and beat at high speed until the mixture is light and fluffy, about 5 minutes. At a drizzle, gradually beat in the vanilla and corn syrup until the filling is the consistency of mayonnaise.

6. Spoon or pipe tablespoon-size blobs of filling onto the flat sides of half the cookies. Flip the remaining cookies on top of the filling, flat side down. Lightly press to form sandwiches.

chocolate-filled PEANUT BUTTER & JELLY SANDWICH cookies

Sandwich cookies are a marvelous thing. Case in point: The Oreo chocolate sandwich is the most popular cookie in the world and has held that status for nearly a century. But as wonderful as the combination of chocolate and vanilla are, nothing, I repeat, nothing can beat chocolate and peanut butter. Except maybe chocolate, peanut butter and jelly.

MAKES 30 SANDWICH COOKIES

$^1/_2$ cup unsalted, roasted peanuts, coarsely chopped

Peanut Butter Sandies (page 197), prepared through step 3

$^1/_4$ cup heavy cream

2 ounces semisweet or bittersweet chocolate, chopped

3 tablespoons unsalted, roasted peanuts, finely chopped

3 tablespoons raspberry jam or preserves

1. Preheat the oven to 375°F.

2. Put the coarsely chopped peanuts in a small bowl. Form rounded teaspoons of dough into balls and dunk half of them into the peanuts. Flatten and round these dough balls out a little, then place them, nut side up, on nonstick or parchment-lined cookie sheets at 2$^1/_2$-inch intervals. With moistened fingers, flatten and round out the remaining (un-nutted) cookies a little. Lay them out on the cookie sheets in 2$^1/_2$-inch intervals.

3. Bake at 375°F. for 11 minutes, or until just set and barely tanned around the edges, turning the cookie sheets around midway through baking. Set the cookies, sheet and all, on a rack to cool.

4. In a small saucepan, cook the cream over medium heat, stirring occasionally, until it just barely starts to boil. Remove from the heat and stir in the chocolate until melted, smooth and blended. Stir in the finely chopped peanuts. Let sit for 20 minutes, until thickened.

5. Flip the cookies that haven't been coated with peanuts (they are the bottoms). Spoon the filling out onto each of the bottom cookies. Spoon or pipe a dab of the jam into the center of the chocolate filling. Place one of the nut-coated cookies on top and lightly press down to form a sandwich.

DOUBLE PEANUT BUTTER CHIP SANDWICHES

These sandwiches are filled with Peanut Butter–Chocolate Chip Buttercream for an extra touch of chocolate and an extra wallop of peanut butter! Prepare the cookies as you would for Chocolate-Filled Peanut Butter & Jelly Sandwich Cookies, then fill with the Buttercream.

PEANUT BUTTER–CHOCOLATE CHIP BUTTERCREAM
½ cup (1 stick) unsalted butter, at room temperature

1 cup creamy peanut butter

1¼ cups confectioners' sugar

3 ounces (½ cup) chocolate morsels

1. Using an electric mixer, beat together the butter and peanut butter at medium speed until blended. Reduce the speed to low and gradually beat in the sugar. Increase the speed to high and beat for 3 minutes, until smooth and fluffy.

2. Flip the cookies that haven't been coated with peanuts. Pipe or spoon teaspoon-size blobs of filling onto them (any tip will work, but an open star tip will give the filling a cute ruffled edge). Sprinkle ½ teaspoon of chocolate morsels on the filling, then lightly press the peanut-coated cookies on top to form sandwiches.

shortnin' bread

Shortnin' bread, or brown sugar shortbread, is the simplest of cookies, but also one of the most satisfying. It's no wonder why Mammy's lil' baby, Pappy's lil' baby and all the grown-up lil' babies love it.

MAKES ABOUT 36 COOKIES

1 cup (2 sticks) unsalted butter, at room temperature
1 cup lightly packed light brown sugar
1 teaspoon vanilla extract and/or bourbon
2½ cups all-purpose flour

1. In a mixing bowl, beat the butter and brown sugar together for 2 minutes, or until fluffy. Beat in the vanilla. Gradually beat in the flour, blending just to combine.

2. Roll the dough out between 2 sheets of waxed paper to a thickness of ¼ inch. Refrigerate on a flat surface for 30 minutes, or until firm.

3. Preheat the oven to 350°F., arranging a rack in the middle position.

4. With a cookie cutter or sharp knife, cut out 1½-inch rounds, or any other shape that you prefer. Transfer the shapes to nonstick or parchment-lined cookie sheets. Refrigerate for 15 minutes (to help the shapes hold).

5. Bake the cookies at 350°F. for 12 minutes, or until lightly tanned around the edges, turning the cookie sheets around midway through baking. Set the cookies, sheet and all, on a rack to cool.

BAKER'S NOTEBOOK

As you cut the little shapes out, you will have little scraps of dough left over. This is sometimes called "negative space." Cut the negative space into little geometric shapes with a small cookie cutter or knife and gently press them on top of your shortnin' bread to make designs.

VARIATION

CHOCOLATE SHORTNIN' BREAD Add 2 tablespoons of unsweetened, Dutch-processed cocoa powder along with the flour to the butter mixture.

nebraska lemon, cornmeal & pecan SHORTBREAD

Out in Nebraska, where the West begins, they bake buttery shortbreads with the tart tang of lemon and true grit of cornmeal. What could be better? How about adding some crunchy pecans? From Omaha to your cookie jar, it's a flavor sensation that can't be beat.

MAKES ABOUT 36 COOKIES

3/4 cup (1 1/2 sticks) unsalted butter, at room temperature

3/4 cup lightly packed light brown sugar

Grated zest of 1 lemon (about 1 tablespoon)

1 large egg

1/2 teaspoon vanilla extract

1/2 teaspoon lemon extract

1/2 cup fine yellow cornmeal

1 3/4 cups all-purpose flour

Egg wash: 1 egg mixed with 2 tablespoons water

1/2 cup chopped pecans

1. In the bowl of an electric mixer, beat the butter, brown sugar and lemon zest at medium speed for 15 seconds, or until smooth. Beat in the egg until completely blended, about 30 seconds. Beat in the vanilla and lemon extracts. Turn the mixer down to its lowest setting and gradually add the cornmeal and flour, blending just to combine.

2. Roll the dough out between 2 sheets of waxed paper to a thickness of 1/4 inch. Refrigerate on a flat surface for 30 minutes, or until firm.

3. Preheat the oven to 350°F., arranging racks in the middle position.

4. With a sharp knife or cookie cutter, cut out 1 1/2-inch shapes and transfer the cookies to a nonstick or parchment-lined cookie sheet. Paint a light coating of egg wash on the cookies and sprinkle with the pecans. Refrigerate for 15 minutes (to help the shapes hold).

5. Bake the cookies at 350°F. for 12 minutes, or until lightly tanned around the edges, turning the cookie sheet midway through baking. Set the cookies, sheet and all, on a rack to cool.

CHOCOLATE-PEANUT biscotti

In 1896, Amedeo Obici, an Italian immigrant, opened a fruit and vegetable stand in Wilkes-Barre, Pennsylvania. What made Amedeo's stand unique was his peanut roaster. Back in those days, roasters had to be hand cranked, but Amedeo came up with a mechanical device that automatically turned the barrel. He also came up with two new flavor sensations: He sprinkled salt on some of the peanuts and dipped others in chocolate. Customers came from all over to nosh on the nuts (well, actually, legumes) so he put up a sign declaring himself "Obici the Peanut Specialist." In 1906, he gave up selling fruit altogether and officially started the Planters Nut & Chocolate Company. Here's a very American version of Italian biscotti, using a combination of ingredients that Obici would surely approve of: peanuts and chocolate.

MAKES ABOUT 24 BISCOTTI

2$^1\!/_2$ cups all-purpose flour

$^1\!/_2$ cup coarse cornmeal, such as buckeye or polenta

1$^1\!/_4$ cups granulated sugar

$^1\!/_2$ cup unsweetened, Dutch-processed cocoa powder

1$^1\!/_2$ teaspoons baking powder

$^1\!/_2$ teaspoon salt

$^3\!/_4$ cup unsalted, roasted peanuts (see page 10)

$^1\!/_2$ cup (1 stick) unsalted butter, at room temperature

2 large eggs

2 tablespoons coffee liqueur (such as Kahlúa) or 1 tablespoon of espresso powder dissolved in 2 tablespoons hot water

1. Preheat the oven to 375°F., arranging a rack in the middle position.

2. Using an electric mixer on low speed, thoroughly combine the flour, cornmeal, sugar, cocoa, baking powder, salt and peanuts. On low speed, add the butter, then the eggs and finally the coffee liqueur. Beat until the dough is thoroughly blended and comes together.

3. Transfer the dough to a lightly floured work surface and shape into a flat log 3 inches wide, 12 inches long and 1 inch high. Place the log on a nonstick or parchment-lined cookie sheet.

4. Bake at 375°F. for 30 minutes, or until set and crusty. Transfer the cookie sheet to a rack to cool for at least 2 hours, or overnight.

5. Preheat the oven to 350°F.

6. Transfer the dough log to a cutting board. With a serrated knife, cut into $\frac{1}{4}$-inch-thick slices and lay them back out on the cookie sheet. Bake at 350°F. for 5 minutes, rotate the cookie sheet front to back, and bake for another 5 to 6 minutes, until toasted. Set the cookies, sheet and all, on a rack to cool.

VARIATION

PECAN BISCOTTI Substitute an extra $\frac{1}{4}$ cup of all-purpose flour for the cocoa and 1 cup of whole pecans for the peanuts. Substitute 2 tablespoons bourbon for the Kahlúa. For a more "European" flavor, substitute 2 tablespoons anisette or sambuca for the Kahlúa.

Vanilla Malt Ice Cream ★ Brown Sugar Ice Cream ★ Milk Chocolate Ice Cream ★ Peanut Butter–Chocolate Crackle Ice Cream ★ Cola Sherbet ★ Raspberry Sherbet ★ Tropical Fruits Foster

ice cream

&

sherbet

Americans have been ice cream fans for quite a while. Even George Washington was fanatical about the stuff. Of course, ice cream is adored all around the world, but Americans have some of the most irresistible methods for enjoying it. We scoop it into a cone, roll it in chocolate sprinkles, drop it into soda pop, swirl it in a blender with milk and malt powder, dip it in chocolate and mount it on the end of a stick. We squash it between two cookies to make a sandwich, smother it in sauces to make sundaes and add it to bananas to make splits. We even coat it in meringue and set it on fire for baked Alaska!

Ice cream can be made in a variety of ways but my favorite method is the one that Reuben Mattus, a Bronx, New York, ice cream maker, reintroduced to America in 1961 when he started Häagen-Dazs. This "French"-style ice cream, or frozen custard, is made with a custard sauce called *crème anglaise*. All of the ice creams in this chapter are made in this rich and creamy manner.

Sherbets are another American favorite. They are simply sorbets smoothed out with a little milk or cream.

Why just have ice cream or sherbet, naked in a bowl, when you can have that wonderful all-American concoction, the sundae? Just scoop your ice cream into a bowl the way you normally would, and then plop on your favorite topping: Chocolate Fudge Sauce (page 243), Simple Chocolate Sauce (page 244), Strawberry Sauce (page 244), plain or Cocoa Whipped Cream (page 250), Wild Berry Whipped Cream (page 251) or Fluffy Marshmallow Sauce (page 249).

TIPS

No matter what the method of operation is, almost every ice cream machine is easy to operate and works well. Just follow the manufacturer's instructions and these helpful hints:

★ **When heating milk and cream, it is important to add a little sugar in the pot. This will help prevent the milk from scorching on the bottom of the pot.**

★ **Make sure to heat milk and cream just to a simmer (it will quiver in the pot and just begin to bubble). Gradually add the hot liquid to the eggs so they are warmed up gradually. This keeps them from scrambling as they are heated.**

★ **Be careful not to let your crème anglaise overcook. Keep everything moving by stirring and scraping the bottom of the pot constantly with a wooden spoon.**

★ **Cool your crème anglaise down in an ice bath to stop the cooking process. If it is slightly curdled, put it in a food processor and process on high for 30 seconds.**

★ **When your ice cream is ready, transfer it to the freezer for a few hours, or overnight, so it can firm up.**

vanilla malt ICE CREAM

Malt, a derivative of barley, adds a deep, mellow flavor to this special vanilla ice cream.

MAKES ABOUT 1 QUART

1 vanilla bean
1½ cups milk
1½ cups heavy cream
¼ cup granulated sugar
¾ cup lightly packed light brown sugar
7 large egg yolks
1 teaspoon vanilla extract
½ cup plain malted milk powder

1. Split the vanilla bean lengthwise and scrape out the seeds. In a medium, heavy-bottomed saucepan, cook the seeds, pod halves, milk, cream and granulated sugar over low heat, stirring occasionally, until the mixture barely starts to boil, 4 to 5 minutes.

2. Put the brown sugar, egg yolks, vanilla extract and malt powder in a large bowl and whisk just to blend. Gradually whisk in the hot cream mixture to warm the egg mixture slowly. Return this crème anglaise mixture to the saucepan. While stirring constantly with a wooden spoon, cook over medium heat until tiny bubbles boil up for 10 seconds. Make sure that you are constantly scraping the spoon across the bottom of the pan so the custard does not scorch. The custard is done when it has thickened slightly and can evenly coat the back of the spoon. Do not let it come to a boil.

3. Strain the custard through a fine sieve. Press out all the liquid in the vanilla beans and nestle the container holding the custard into a large bowl of ice. Let cool, stirring occasionally.

4. Transfer to an ice cream machine and freeze according to the manufacturer's instructions. Put the finished ice cream in a storage container and freeze until firm.

VARIATION

CLASSIC VANILLA ICE CREAM Just omit the malt powder.

BROWN SUGAR ice cream

Molasses and dark brown sugar have been American favorites since Colonial times. A little vanilla extract mellows out their flavor and gives this ice cream a magically rich taste.

MAKES ABOUT 1 QUART

1½ cups milk

1½ cups heavy cream

1 tablespoon granulated sugar

1 cup lightly packed dark brown sugar

7 large egg yolks

1 teaspoon vanilla extract

2 tablespoons unsulphured molasses

1. In a medium, heavy-bottomed saucepan, cook the milk, cream and granulated sugar over low heat, stirring occasionally, until the mixture just barely starts to boil, 4 to 5 minutes.

2. Put the brown sugar, egg yolks, vanilla extract and molasses in a large bowl and whisk just to blend. Gradually whisk in the hot cream mixture to warm the egg mixture slowly. Return this crème anglaise mixture to the saucepan. While constantly stirring with a wooden spoon, cook over medium heat until tiny bubbles boil up for 10 seconds. Make sure that you are constantly scraping the spoon across the bottom of the pan so the custard does not scorch. The custard is done when it has thickened slightly and can evenly coat the back of the spoon. Do not let it come to a boil.

3. Strain the custard through a fine sieve and nestle the container holding the custard into a large bowl of ice. Let cool, stirring occasionally.

4. Transfer to an ice cream machine and freeze according to the manufacturer's instructions. Put the finished ice cream in a storage container and freeze until firm.

milk chocolate ICE CREAM

A little malt really brings out the flavor of milk chocolate in this extra creamy ice cream. This frozen treat is wonderful when paired with Vanilla Malt Ice Cream (page 230) or Classic Vanilla Ice Cream (page 230). For even more of a taste sensation, add one of your favorite toppings (see page 228) and a generous dollop of chopped nuts, fresh berries, toasted coconut or multicolored sprinkles. And don' t forget the cherry on top!

MAKES ABOUT 1 QUART

6 ounces milk chocolate

1¹⁄₂ cups milk

1¹⁄₂ cups heavy cream

¹⁄₄ cup plus 2 tablespoons granulated sugar

7 large egg yolks

1 teaspoon vanilla extract

1 tablespoon malt powder

1. Melt the chocolate in a completely dry bowl or double boiler set over barely simmering water.

2. In a medium, heavy-bottomed saucepan, cook the milk, cream and 2 tablespoons of the sugar over low heat, stirring occasionally, until the mixture just barely starts to boil, about 4 to 5 minutes.

3. Put the remainder of the sugar, the egg yolks, vanilla extract and malt powder in a large bowl and whisk just to blend. Gradually whisk in the hot cream mixture to warm the egg mixture slowly. Return this crème anglaise mixture to the saucepan. While constantly stirring with a wooden spoon, cook over medium heat until tiny bubbles boil up for 10 seconds. Make sure that you are constantly scraping the spoon across the bottom of the pan so the custard does not scorch. The custard is done when it has thickened slightly and can evenly coat the back of the spoon. Do not let it come to a boil.

4. Strain the custard through a fine sieve and whisk in the melted chocolate until smooth. Nestle the container holding the custard into a large bowl of ice. Let the custard cool, stirring occasionally.

5. Transfer to an ice cream machine and freeze according to the manufacturer's instructions. Put the finished ice cream in a storage container and freeze until firm.

There are many accounts of how and where the ice cream sundae was invented and named. It is alleged that it was invented in 1881, at Ed Berner's Ice Cream Parlor in Two Rivers, Wisconsin, when a customer named George Hallauer requested that some chocolate syrup be poured over his ice cream. It is also claimed that the name sundae was coined by George Guffy, who served them only on Sunday because ice cream sodas were banned on that day.

PEANUT BUTTER-CHOCOLATE CRACKLE ice cream

Peanut butter and chocolate are a winning combination. You can use chocolate morsels, but they are a poor substitute for these thin chocolate crackles. Morsels just seem to squash in your mouth and stay too cold to release their flavor. The crackles stay crisp and crunchy, then melt on your tongue to release all their chocolaty goodness.

MAKES ABOUT 1 QUART

1$\frac{1}{2}$ cups milk

1$\frac{1}{2}$ cups heavy cream

1 cup granulated sugar

7 large egg yolks

1$\frac{1}{4}$ cups creamy peanut butter

4 ounces bittersweet chocolate, coarsely chopped

1. In a medium, heavy-bottomed saucepan, cook the milk, cream and $\frac{1}{4}$ cup of the sugar over low heat, stirring occasionally, until the mixture just barely starts to boil, 4 to 5 minutes.

2. Put the remaining $\frac{3}{4}$ cup sugar and the egg yolks in a large bowl and whisk just to blend. Gradually whisk in the hot cream mixture to warm the egg mixture slowly. Return this crème anglaise mixture to the saucepan. While stirring constantly with a wooden spoon, cook over medium heat until tiny bubbles boil up for 10 seconds. Make sure that you are constantly scraping the spoon across the bottom of the pan so the custard does not scorch. The custard is done when it has thickened slightly and can evenly coat the back of the spoon. Do not let it come to a boil.

3. Strain the custard through a fine sieve and stir in the peanut butter until smooth and melted. Nestle the container holding the custard into a large bowl of ice. Let cool, stirring occasionally.

4. Transfer to an ice cream machine and freeze according to the manufacturer's instructions.

5. Melt the chocolate in a completely dry bowl or double boiler set over barely simmering water. Remove from the heat and let cool slightly, but don't let it harden.

6. When the ice cream is done but still soft, transfer it to a cold bowl. Hold a rubber spatula in one hand and a spoon in the other. While folding the ice cream with the rubber spatula, drizzle a fine ribbon of melted chocolate into it with the spoon. Fold all of the chocolate in streaks into the ice cream. Put the finished ice cream in a storage container and freeze until firm.

VARIATION

PEANUT BUTTER-MILK CHOCOLATE CRACKLE ICE CREAM

Follow the instructions above, but after using the ice cream machine, do not freeze the ice cream to harden immediately. Using 2 ounces of milk chocolate instead of the bittersweet chocolate, follow steps 5 and 6 of this recipe to drizzle melted milk chocolate into the milk chocolate ice cream.

> In about 1920, Christian Kent Nelson, a high school science teacher in Iowa, figured out how to coat a block of ice cream with chocolate. At first, the product was called an "I-Scream-Bar," but the name was soon changed to Eskimo Pie in 1921, when Nelson joined forces with candymaker Russell C. Stover to produce and distribute the treat nationally.

COLA sherbet

In 1886, Atlanta pharmacist John Pemberton allegedly combined cola nut and coca leaf extracts into a pleasant-tasting syrup for curing hangovers. He cooked it all up in a big iron kettle in his backyard and stirred it with an oar. Soon he was selling it to other Atlanta pharmacists, one of whom tried it mixed with soda water. A few years later, Asa G. Candler bought the formula for two thousand dollars, and the rest is soft-drink history.

I am always puzzled as to why cola is so rarely used in desserts. After all, it is one of the most popular flavors in America. It makes a great, and easy-to-make, sherbet. If you don' t have an ice cream maker, freeze it in a shallow container and chop it up with a fork to make a cola granita.

MAKES ABOUT 6 CUPS

1 quart cola
¾ cup granulated sugar
1 cup light cream
1 cup half-and-half

1. In a medium saucepan, heat 1 cup of the cola and all of the sugar until the sugar crystals dissolve. Set aside to cool, then whisk in the rest of the cola, the cream, and half-and-half.

2. Transfer to an ice cream machine and freeze according to the manufacturer's instructions. Put the finished sherbet in a storage container and freeze until firm.

VARIATION

Try substituting root beer, cream soda or any of your favorite sodas for the cola.

raspberry SHERBET

Summertime, when berries are cheap, plentiful and at the peak of their flavor, is the right time to make a nice, cool berry sherbet like this one. If you see slightly bruised or overripe berries being offered at a bargain price, be sure to buy them. They're perfect for this luscious sorbet.

MAKES ABOUT 5 CUPS

4 half-pints fresh raspberries or 2 12-ounce packages of frozen raspberries
½ cup granulated sugar
1 cup half-and-half

1. In a covered saucepan, bring the raspberries, 1 cup of water and the sugar to a boil, then simmer for 3 minutes. Let cool, then strain, pressing out as much of the juice and pulp as possible. Whisk in the half-and-half.

2. Transfer to an ice cream maker and freeze according to the manufacturer's instructions. Put the finished sherbet in a storage container and freeze until firm.

VARIATIONS

EXOTIC BERRY SHERBET Substitute blackberries, marionberries or golden or black raspberries for the raspberries.

BLACK RASPBERRY SHERBET Since genuine black raspberries are quite hard to come by, substitute 2 pints raspberries and 2 pints blackberries for a wonderful, ersatz version.

tropical fruits FOSTER

With its mix of French, Spanish, African and American cultures, New Orleans is one of the most unique culinary melting pots in the world. It all started when a contingent of cooking school graduates (sent over as mail-order brides) arrived in the Colonial outpost of Louisiana. Far from France, they had to create new recipes with whatever was on hand. In 1799, the development of new methods for refining sugarcane established the city as a sugar-producing center. This led to the creation of all sorts of local confections and desserts. In the 1800s, pecan and toffee lollipops were sold on street corners. Today, no visit is complete without a trip to the candy store for some pecan pralines. Ever since the Café des Emigrés opened in 1791, "The Big Easy" has been famous for its French Quarter restaurants. At Brennan's, the signature dessert of flambéed bananas and ice cream was named after one of their regular customers, Mr. Foster. Here is a tropical twist on this classic New Orleans dessert.

SERVES 4 TO 6

4 tablespoons unsalted butter

$\frac{1}{2}$ cup lightly packed dark brown sugar

2 bananas, peeled and sliced

$\frac{1}{2}$ pineapple, peeled, cored and cut into $\frac{1}{4}$-inch wedges

1 mango, peeled and pitted and cut in $\frac{1}{4}$-inch slices

$\frac{1}{4}$ cup dark rum, preferably Jamaican

$\frac{1}{2}$ cup heavy cream

1 pint Classic Vanilla Ice Cream (page 230), Vanilla Malt Ice Cream (page 230)
   or Brown Sugar Ice Cream (page 231)

1. In a large sauté pan set over medium-high heat, cook and stir the butter and brown sugar until they combine into a smooth syrup. Add the bananas, pineapple and mango, coat the fruit with the syrup, and cook for 1 minute more.

2. Carefully pour in the rum. If it does not burst into flames spontaneously, ignite with a match. Gently swirl the pan and baste the bananas until the flames die out.

3. Add the cream and cook for 1 more minute.

4. Divide the fruit and sauce among serving bowls. Add a scoop of ice cream to each. Serve at once.

Use caution. Flambéed desserts can be dangerous!
- **Make sure that nothing flammable is near the pan.**
- **Never pour straight from the bottle. Measure out flammable liquids into a small pitcher.**
- **Stand back when adding alcohol to a hot pan.**

Chocolate Fudge Sauce ★ **Simple Chocolate Sauce** ★ **Strawberry Sauce** ★ **Lemon Buttermilk Custard Sauce** ★ **Brown Sugar Custard Sauce** ★ **Whiskey & Molasses Sauce** ★ **Orange Hard Sauce** ★ **Fluffy Marshmallow Sauce** ★ **Whipped Cream** ★ **Cocoa Whipped Cream** ★ **Wild Berry Whipped Cream**

sauces & toppings

A piece of cake or a portion of pudding is wonderful on its own, but with a little dessert sauce, it becomes absolutely fabulous. Americans like dessert sauces, especially on ice cream, cobblers and puddings, and they like them thick, rich and full of flavor, from that American classic, Chocolate Fudge Sauce, to cloudlike dollops of Fluffy Marshmallow Sauce.

TIPS

These sauces are enchantingly easy and remarkably good. Here are a few tips to make the process even smoother.

★ While sauces are cooking, scrape the bottom of the pan with a whisk or spoon to prevent scorching. Don't just stir. You should be able to feel the pressure of the whisk or spoon as it rubs against the bottom.

★ When using a candy thermometer, always bend down to read the mercury at eye level. This will give you a much more accurate reading of the temperature.

★ If chocolate sauce solidifies in the refrigerator, place the container in hot water to slowly melt.

CHOCOLATE FUDGE sauce

Many sauces claim to be fudge but this one is the real McCoy! It is thick, sticky and full of chocolate flavor. Spoon it over ice cream to create a sensational hot fudge sundae.

MAKES 2 CUPS

3/4 cup freshly brewed, hot coffee

1/4 cup granulated sugar

1/4 cup unsweetened, Dutch-processed, cocoa powder

1/2 cup light corn syrup

4 ounces semisweet chocolate, chopped

1. In a small saucepan, cook the coffee and sugar together over medium-high heat until all the sugar crystals are dissolved, about 3 minutes. Remove from the heat and whisk in the cocoa. Add the corn syrup and whisk until the mixture is completely smooth.

2. Place the semisweet chocolate in a dry, medium bowl over barely simmering water and stir occasionally until melted. Whisk the melted chocolate into the coffee-cocoa mixture until smooth and blended. The sauce is best if refrigerated for a full day before serving.

3. To serve, heat the sauce in a small bowl or double boiler set over simmering water, stirring occasionally, until warm.

simple CHOCOLATE SAUCE

This is an incredibly easy-to-make sauce with a two-fisted wallop of chocolate flavor. It will take any chocolate dessert up a notch.

MAKES ABOUT 1 CUP

4 ounces semisweet chocolate
¾ cup freshly brewed coffee

Put the chocolate in a small bowl. In a small saucepan, bring the coffee to a simmer, then pour over the chocolate. Working from the center out, gently stir with a whisk to melt and blend. Continue stirring until smooth. Let sit for 15 minutes to thicken.

STRAWBERRY sauce

Here's a refreshing pick-me-up sauce for ice cream or puddings. It's a great way to use damaged or bruised strawberries.

MAKES 2 CUPS

1 pint strawberries
½ cup granulated sugar
1 tablespoon elderberry cordial or orange liqueur (optional)

Wash and hull the strawberries. Put them in a food processor with the sugar and the cordial, if using. Process until liquefied.

LEMON BUTTERMILK
custard sauce

Lemon and buttermilk add a refreshing zip to this creamy custard sauce. Use it with any berry or stone-fruit dessert.

MAKES 1¹/₂ CUPS

¹/₂ cup granulated sugar
¹/₄ cup fresh lemon juice
¹/₂ cup milk
¹/₄ cup heavy cream
4 large egg yolks
1 teaspoon vanilla extract
¹/₂ cup buttermilk

1. In a small saucepan over medium heat, bring ¹/₄ cup of the sugar and the lemon juice to a boil. Continue to boil, stirring occasionally, for 1 minute, or until the crystals dissolve. Set the lemon syrup aside to cool.

2. In a medium saucepan, cook the milk and cream over medium heat, stirring occasionally, until the mixture just barely starts to boil, about 3 minutes.

3. Put the yolks, vanilla and remaining ¹/₄ cup of sugar in a medium bowl and whisk just to blend. Gradually whisk in the hot cream mixture to warm the yolk mixture slowly. Return the mixture to the saucepan and cook over low heat, constantly stirring and scraping the bottom of the pan, until tiny bubbles boil up continuously for 10 seconds.

4. Strain the custard through a fine sieve into a bowl. Stir in the buttermilk and lemon syrup. Nestle the bowl in ice until cool.

brown sugar CUSTARD SAUCE

The robust flavor of molasses turns rich and mellow in this custardy sauce. It goes perfectly with warm cobblers and puddings.

MAKES 1½ CUPS

1 vanilla bean
½ cup milk
½ cup heavy cream
1 tablespoon granulated sugar
¼ cup lightly packed light brown sugar
3 large egg yolks
1 teaspoon vanilla extract
1 tablespoon molasses

1. Split the vanilla bean lengthwise and scrape out the seeds. In a medium, heavy-bottomed saucepan, cook the seeds, pod halves, milk, cream and granulated sugar over low heat, stirring occasionally, until the mixture just barely starts to boil, 3 to 4 minutes.

2. Put the brown sugar, egg yolks and vanilla extract in a medium bowl and whisk just to blend. Gradually whisk in the hot cream mixture to warm the egg mixture slowly. Return the mixture to the saucepan and cook over low heat, constantly stirring and scraping the bottom of the pan, until tiny bubbles boil up continuously for 10 seconds.

3. Strain through a fine sieve into a bowl, then stir in the molasses. Nestle the bowl in ice until cool.

WHISKEY & MOLASSES sauce

This sauce is a classic accompaniment to bread pudding, but it will add a sticky and gooey dimension to any simple cake or pudding.

MAKES 1¼ CUPS

4 tablespoons unsalted butter
1 cup lightly packed dark brown sugar
½ cup bourbon
1 cup heavy cream
¼ cup molasses
1 teaspoon vanilla extract

In a medium saucepan over medium-high heat, melt the butter and brown sugar together. Carefully pour in the bourbon. If it does not burst into flames spontaneously, carefully ignite with a match. The liquid will flame until the alcohol burns off. Add the cream and cook for 5 more minutes, until thickened. Stir in the molasses and vanilla. Strain the sauce and let it cool.

Use caution. Flambéed desserts can be dangerous!
- **Make sure that nothing flammable is near the pan.**
- **Never pour straight from the bottle. Measure out flammable liquids into a small pitcher.**
- **Stand back when adding alcohol to a hot pan.**

orange HARD SAUCE

Here's a buttery orange sauce that should be served slightly chilled and still solid. The trick is to use it on a warm pudding, cake or pie. It quickly melts into a luscious sauce.

For even quicker melting, pop the whole dessert into a preheated oven until the sauce is halfway melted, then serve.

MAKES 1½ CUPS

½ cup (1 stick) unsalted butter, at room temperature

1½ cups confectioners' sugar

Grated zest of 1 orange (2 to 3 tablespoons)

1 teaspoon vanilla extract

¼ cup orange liqueur

1. Using an electric mixer, beat together the butter, sugar and orange zest until very light and creamy, about 3 minutes. Gradually beat in the vanilla and the orange liqueur.

2. Fit a pastry bag with a half-inch star tip and fill the bag with the sauce. Pipe individual, tablespoon-size portions onto waxed paper. Refrigerate for at least 2 hours, then remove from the refrigerator 10 minutes before serving.

fluffy MARSHMALLOW SAUCE

Here's a sauce that's at home on top of your favorite ice cream or in the middle of a peanut butter sandwich. In reality, it has nothing whatsoever to do with marshmallows.

MAKES ABOUT 2 CUPS

½ cup light corn syrup
½ cup granulated sugar
2 large egg whites
Pinch of salt
Pinch of cream of tartar
1 teaspoon vanilla extract

1. In a small saucepan, bring ¼ cup of water, the corn syrup and all but 1 tablespoon of the sugar to 246°F. (firm-ball stage).

2. In the completely clean and dry bowl of an electric mixer, whisk the egg whites, salt and cream of tartar until creamy and foamy. Still whisking, sprinkle in the remaining tablespoon of sugar and continue to whisk until the whites hold very soft peaks. With the mixer on low, carefully drizzle in the hot syrup. Turn the mixer to high and whisk until thick, fluffy and just warm, about 7 minutes. Turn the mixer to low and whisk in the vanilla extract.

whipped cream

Here's a good standby recipe for whipped cream. Pick any of the suggested flavorings to match your dessert. Maraschino, an Italian dark cherry liqueur, is my personal favorite.

MAKES ABOUT 4 CUPS WHIPPED CREAM

2 cups heavy or whipping cream

3 tablespoons confectioners' sugar

1 tablespoon bourbon, dark rum, maraschino (cherry) liqueur, orange liqueur
   or 1 teaspoon vanilla extract

In a large, chilled bowl, whip the cream until slightly thickened. Add the sugar and liquor or liqueur. Whip to the consistency of shaving cream.

cocoa WHIPPED CREAM

This deep chocolate whipped cream is so luscious you could almost serve it on its own. Use it to top any chocolate dessert.

MAKES ABOUT 4 CUPS WHIPPED CREAM

$\frac{1}{2}$ cup confectioners' sugar

2 cups heavy or whipping cream

$\frac{1}{4}$ cup unsweetened cocoa powder

1. Sift the confectioners' sugar into a sheet of waxed paper.

2. In a large, chilled bowl, whip the cream, cocoa and sugar to the consistency of shaving cream.

WILD BERRY whipped cream

This is a great way to use berries that are bruised or otherwise on the way out. Just make sure they are not moldy. You may use any combination of berries or preserves for this yummy concoction.

MAKES ABOUT 4 CUPS WHIPPED CREAM

2 tablespoons granulated sugar

$^1/_2$ pint fresh raspberries, blackberries, blueberries, or other berries, or 6 ounces of Individually Quick Frozen (IQF) raspberries

$^1/_4$ cup raspberry, blueberry or mixed berry preserves

2 cups heavy or whipping cream

$^1/_4$ cup confectioners' sugar

1. Put the sugar and berries in a saucepan with 1 tablespoon of water, cover and bring to a boil over low heat. Simmer for 2 minutes, or until the berries soften. Stir in the preserves, cover again, and cook until melted. Remove from the heat, pass through a fine strainer to remove the pips and refrigerate until chilled.

2. In a chilled bowl, whip the cream, berry mixture and confectioners' sugar to soft, fluffy peaks.

Many people must be thanked for their contribution to the making of this book. If I could show my appreciation by holding a ticker-tape parade down Broadway, I would, but New York traffic and parking regulations make this a little prohibitive. Instead, I will bestow this statement of thanks. My gratitude 'tis of thee:

First is my all-seeing and all-knowing editor, Pam Krauss, and her constantly on-the-ball assistant editor, Adina Steiman. Jane Treuhaft, who designed the book, never seemed to run out of brilliantly creative ideas and concepts (check out that cover—is that great, or what?). Photographer Tina Rupp had an amazing take on every shot; it was a delight to work with her.

The recipes in this book took years to both research and rework. Developing them has been an ongoing project as I worked in several food venues. Thanks for help and inspiration go to restaurant colleagues: John McFadden, Rob Ubhaus, Chris Randell, Liza Rivera and Amanda Barnes. Special thanks to BR Guest Pastry Chef Lincoln Carson. (Linc was always there with encyclopedic information.) Thanks to the crew at Food Network, who are always lending support: Irene Wong, Marc Dissen, Bob Tuschman, Michael Simon and Gale Gand, with very, very special thanks to Sara Moulton. Thanks also to Brian Maynard of KitchenAid and Chris Terri of Calphalon.

Very special kudos must go out to some fellow champions of the American dessert. They have been active in elevating the status of American baking to the respected position it holds today. I thank them for the support and guidance they have given to me throughout my career: Michael Batterberry of *Food Arts,* Michael Schneider of *Chocolatier,* Gael Greene of *New York* magazine and Bobby Flay of Mesa Grill.

Special mention to the late Richard Sax, whose work first inspired me to rediscover so many great American desserts.

Thanks and love to my wife, Jacqueline, and two daughters, Isabella and Violet. They endured Daddy's constant working and editing, and were also invaluable in the oh-so-important task of recipe tasting.

Finally, a thank-you that extends from the purple mountain majesties to the oceans white with foam for my friend, confidante, guru and literary agent, Jane Dystel.

index